In Time O

CW00959620

In Time O' Strife

original script by
Joe Corrie

adaptation by
Graham McLaren

B L O O M S B U R Y
LONDON · NEW DELHI · NEW YORK · SYDNEY

Bloomsbury Methuen Drama

An imprint of Bloomsbury Publishing Plc

50 Bedford Square	1385 Broadway
London	New York
WC1B 3DP	NY 10018
UK	USA

www.bloomsbury.com

Bloomsbury is a registered trade mark of Bloomsbury Publishing Plc

First published 1926
Published by 7:84 Theatre Company 1982
First published by Bloomsbury Methuen Drama 2013

In Time O' Strife © The Estate of Joe Corrie
In Time O' Strife adapted by Graham McLaren 2013

Photographs © Eoin Carey

British Library Cataloguing-in-Publication Data
A catalogue record for this book is available from the British Library.

Library of Congress Cataloging-in-Publication Data
A catalog record for this book is available from the Library of Congress.

ISBN: PB: 978-1-4725-2243-6
ePDF: 978-1-4725-2374-7
ePub: 978-1-4725-3041-7

Typeset by Country Setting, Kingsdown, Kent CT14 8ES

Contents

Joe Corrie was a Scottish miner, poet and playwright. Corrie began his writing career providing poetry, articles and short stories for a number of prominent socialist newspapers and journals. By the late 1920s he had begun to be regarded as a poet of great promise: 'The Image O' God and Other Poems' was enormously successful and was quickly followed by several other volumes.

Corrie first turned his attention to writing plays during the General Strike of May 1926. During this time he wrote his first full-length play, *In Time O' Strife*, which became a huge success, touring Scottish mining villages and music halls. Following this Corrie went on to write extensively for the Scottish Community Drama Association (SCDA).

During his career, Corrie's first concern and commitment lay with the Scottish working classes. He used his playwriting abilities to portray something of their lives and experience and to involve them in the production of the play.

Provided courtesy of Linda Mackenney

Graham McLaren is a Glasgow-based theatre artist who has been making theatre for almost two decades. In that time he has created work ranging from totally improvised and devised work to classical texts. He has made shows in London's West End, ancient Greek amphitheatres, national theatres and festivals across the world. In 1994, he established the internationally acclaimed Theatre Babel, where he remained Artistic Director until 2008. In 2005, Graham was invited to join Perth Theatre, Scotland, as Artistic and Co-Creative Director; he remained with Perth Theatre until January 2008. The following year he began creating work for the Toronto-based theatre company Necessary Angel as Associate Artist. He is currently an Associate Director of the National Theatre of Scotland, where his previous shows include *A Doll's House*, *A Christmas Carol* and *Men Should Weep*.

Foreword

Joe Corrie, my father, wrote *In Time O' Strife* from the Fife coalfields at the end of the 1926 miners' strike/lockout. A miner himself, he was one of the unemployed. The strike began after the coal-owners had announced their intention to reduce miners' pay and increase their working hours to compensate for falling profits caused partly by the availability of cheap German coal from reparation at the end of the First World War. The miners' unions refused. They were supported for the first nine days by the General Strike, then they were on their own, and seven months of hardship resulted. There were soup kitchens and a certain amount of Parish Relief, as you will read in the play, but the latter was nowhere near even the low wages the miners had received. By November they could hold out no longer and returned to work on the new terms. The play describes the hardships and the temptation of some men to break strike in the face of their wives' fierce insistence not to do so.

My father had been writing since about 1918 and became known locally as 'the poet'. One satirical poem, 'It's Fine tae Keep in wi' the Gaffer', got him into trouble, but fortunately not to the extent of losing his job. He began to contribute articles and poems to socialist newspapers, one of which published them. These were initially lyrics before he moved to hard realism.

During the lock-out, he wrote one-act plays, mostly comedies, and started an amateur dramatic society from among friends and neighbours, who performed at local concerts to help fund soup kitchens. *In Time O' Strife* was his first full-length play. He toured it from 1928 until about 1931 with the amateur company, first to village halls in Fife, as the Bowhill Players, then – with a professional theatre manager who saw one of their performances and renamed them the Fife Miner Players – to theatres throughout Scotland, along with sketches such as *Hogmanay* and *The Shillin' a Week Man*.

In 1930 *In Time O' Strife* was produced by an actors' collective in Leipzig and my father went to see it. I haven't been able to trace how they heard about it, but the event merits retelling. The company played it in tandem with *Wunder um Verdun* (*The Miracle at Verdun*), a symbolical pacifist play by Hans Chlumberg. Born in 1897, Chlumberg (full name Hans Bardach Edler von Chlumberg) was an Austrian aristocrat who'd attended military college and served in the war as a cavalry lieutenant. A meeting between the two playwrights would have been interesting. It didn't happen, because Chlumberg was killed when he fell into the orchestra pit during a rehearsal. The company intended that the more popular of the plays would tour, and that turned out to be Chlumberg's. It was translated into English and other languages and produced in London's West End and in New York. Aaron Copland wrote incidental music for that production.

After the touring players, my father followed the life of a freelance writer of poems, plays and some journalism. He was probably best known in the amateur drama movement, for which he wrote many one-act plays.

To go back to 1926: as elsewhere in British coalfields, the miners in Fife lived in 'miners' rows' of two-roomed houses, usually built by the coal companies, with outside lavatories and pumps in the street for water. The rows had numbers instead of names and this, in a way, symbolised their apartness from the wider community. It had been like this for centuries. The other side of the coin is that living together fostered a spirit which kept them going during the lock-out. All these aspects appear in the play.

So how did a boy who had left school at fourteen to work in the local pit know about poems and plays, and how to write them? First of all came the urge to write. Then he claimed that his education was thorough in the three 'r's. Certainly, his grammar and general use of language were perfect. He saw plays from childhood when the Penny Geggies visited. These touring troupes of actors came to the mining villages in caravans, set up booths with seating and a stage, and performed both Shakespeare and melodramas like *East Lynne* and *Maria Martin and the Murder in the Red Barn.* Admission cost pennies and, in the case of children, probably empty jam jars and bottles. My father was allowed to help behind the scenes.

Books probably came from the Bowhill recreation and reading room which had opened in 1904. There was also the company of like-minded, often older, men. As my father wrote many years later:

> I was living in a locality where there was a good deal of intelligence, political consciousness, and rebelliousness against the many iniquities of the coal industry. We had an excellent library and reading room, and literature was discussed a good deal as we walked the country roads in groups. These indeed were days to be remembered with pleasure.

On this positive note I pass you on to the play.

Morag Corrie
October 2013

In Time O' Strife

The 1926 text by Joe Corrie

Characters

Jock Smith, *a miner*
Jean Smith, *his wife*
Jenny Smith, *their daughter, twenty-two*
Lizzie Smith, *their daughter, thirteen*
Bob Smith, *their son, seventeen*
Tam Pettigrew, *a miner*
Agnes Pettigrew, *his wife*
Kate Pettigrew, *their daughter, twenty-two*
Tam Anderson, *a young miner*
Wull Baxter, *a young miner*

Act One

The kitchen of the Smiths' home in the mining village of Carhill, in Scotland.

A bed, heavily curtained, occupies almost the whole of the left side of the room (from the spectators' viewpoint). A dresser covered with nick-nacks stands at back. To the right of the dresser is a four-paned window through which can be seen the colliery in the distance.

The table stands in the centre of floor.

Between dresser and window is a stool, on which stands the water pail and a tinnie.

The door leading to the outside is at left back. The door to room is right back.

The time is night, and the lamp has been lit and window curtains drawn. The period of the play is the mining crisis of 1926.

At rise of curtain, **Lizzie***, pencil in her mouth, is on her knees on a chair at the tableside, poring over her home lessons.*

Jenny *sits at fireside, converting an old hat into a new one with a piece of ribbon.*

The sound of marching people can be heard singing:

> We'll hang every blackleg to the sour apple tree,
> We'll hang every blackleg to the sour apple tree,
> We'll hang every blackleg to the sour apple tree,
> As we go marching on.

The tune is 'John Brown's Body'. When they have faded away in the distance –

Lizzie (*sings*)
> We'll hang every blackleg to the sour apple tree,
> We'll hang every blackleg to the sour apple tree,
> We'll hang every blackleg to the sour apple tree,
> As we go marching . . .

Jenny   Here! You get thae sums done.

Lizzie (*shortly*)   I canna dae them, you better ha'e a shot at them, Jenny.

Jenny   What kind are they, thae kind wi' the dots?

Lizzie   Ay.

Jenny   Weel, you'll need to try Bob.

Lizzie   Bob! He canna dae decimals . . . I'll get the strap the morn if I dinna ha'e them done.

Jenny   Let him try and gi'e you the strap, and there'll be some fun.

Lizzie   He's done it before.

Jenny   Ay, but there's a strike on noo, and we're lookin' for blood. But does he no' let you see hoo to dae your sums?

Lizzie   Ay, but he thinks we're a' as clever as him. I wish I was awa' frae the schule, Jenny, I dinna like it.

Jenny   We a' wish we were awa' frae the schule, but we're no' lang till we wish we were back to it.

Singing of crowd can be faintly heard in the distance.

Lizzie   Is the strike aboot finished, Jenny?

Jenny   God knows. It was as like finishin' six weeks ago as it is the day.

Lizzie   Will we ha'e ony tea the nicht before we go to bed?

Jenny   I'll be able to tell you that at bedtime. Get your lessons done.

Lizzie   It's no' easy daen' lessons when you're hungry.

(*Sings.*)

> We'll hang every blackleg to the sour apple tree,
> We'll hang every blackleg to the sour apple tree,
> We'll hang every . . .

Jenny   Shut it! D'ye want to wauken him?

Jenny *nods her head in direction of room. The door opens, and* **Agnes Pettigrew** *enters. She is rather shabby, and there is the look of illness on her face. She walks wearily, and is troubled with a little, harsh cough.*

Agnes   Is your mither in, Jenny?

Jenny   No, she's awa' doon the street, Auntie . . . Sit doon.

Agnes *sits at left side of table.*

Jenny   What's a' the noise aboot the nicht?

Agnes   I dinna ken. There's been a meetin' in the hall aboot something. Oor Tam'll no' go to the meetin's to let us ken what's gaun on.

Lizzie   Can you dae sums, Auntie?

Jenny   Here! Shut that book till Bob comes in!

Lizzie   Bob canna dae them.

Jenny   Weel, awa' to the schoolmaister and get him to do them, that's what he's gettin' paid for.

Agnes *coughs.*

Jenny   That cauld's no' leavin' you in a hurry, Auntie.

Agnes   No . . . It's no' sae bad in the daytime, but it keeps me off my sleep at nicht.

Jenny   Ha'e ye seen the doctor yet?

Agnes   What guid would he dae? He'd just order me to my bed, and gi'e me a line for medicine. And what guid is that when there's no' a penny in the house?

Jenny   It's true, Auntie.

Lizzie   I wish the strike was finished till I get my new frock.

Jenny   Where is Kate the nicht, Auntie?

Agnes   She's sittin' mendin' wee Wullie's troosers. I think she's gaun to the soup-kitchen dance the nicht.

Jenny   She's lucky. A nicht's dancin' noo and I'd ha'e nae shoon left. Anither month o' this strike and we'll be gaun aboot as naked as savages.

Agnes   It canna last much langer noo, Jenny, it canna, or the half o' us'll gang mad.

Jenny   This is the worst week we have had; it'll be the same wi' you, I suppose?

Agnes   I dinna ken hoo to turn, Jenny; we're clean knocked oot. We'll need to hunger noo till we get the Pairish relief the morn . . . I'm gettin' tired, Jenny.

Jenny   The strike canna last lang noo, Auntie, and twa weeks' work'll put us on oor feet again.

Agnes   We've been sayin' that for the last twa months, but the end doesna seem to be ony nearer.

She takes a fit of coughing. **Jenny** *goes to her, and gives her a drink of water.*

Jenny   You'll need to see the doctor, Auntie, that cough's gettin' worse.

Agnes   Ay, I'll need to see him, Jenny. But I'll wait a day or twa . . . If he puts me to my bed I'll never rise again, I doot.

Jenny   That's nonsense: he'll gi'e ye a bottle that'll stop that cough in a nicht . . . You should ha'e mair claes on tae.

Agnes   Mair claes! (*She laughs hysterically.*) Mair claes! . . . I wonder if I'll get a sleep the nicht? . . . When the cough does stop I canna sleep for thinkin' on the bairns.

Jenny   You'll need to stop thinkin' o' the bairns.

Agnes   That's no' easy, Jenny, when you're a mither you'll see that . . . Puir wee things, they seem to ken, for they just sit and look like wee lambs and never say a word when I've to put them to bed to sleep the hunger of them. (*She holds her brow with her hand.*) Jenny, I'm no' weel.

Jenny   I ken you're no' weel, it's your bed you should be in. Kate can look after the bairns weel enough.

Agnes   I'm feart to go to bed. I ha'e the feelin' that if I lie doon . . . (*Rises.*) Ach: God kens what we have been broucht on the face o' this earth for.

Jenny   You get awa' doon hame, and ha'e rest for a while. A guid nicht's sleep, and you'll be like anither woman in the mornin'.

Agnes (*going off*)   Peace! . . . Peace! . . . I wonder when we'll ever get peace?

She goes out coughing. **Jenny** *goes with her.*

Lizzie (*singing*)
    We'll hang every blackleg to the sour apple tree,
    We'll hang every blackleg to the sour apple tree,
    We'll hang every blackleg to the sour –

Jock (*loudly from room*)   Shut up in there!

Lizzie *shuts up suddenly, and puts her finger in her mouth.*

Jenny *re-enters.*

Jenny   Was that him shoutin'?

Lizzie   No.

Jenny   It's a wonder he hasna been cryin' for water.

Enter **Bob**, *a reckless kind of youth, light of foot as an Irish ragman.*

Bob   What aboot some chuck?

Jenny   What aboot it?

Bob   Weel, what aboot it?

Jenny   You'll need to rin and play hide and seek till my mither comes hame – and mebbe efter she comes hame tae.

Lizzie   Can you dae decimals, Bob?

Bob   Can I dae what?

Lizzie   Decimals?

Bob   What's decimals?

Lizzie   Sums, fathead.

Bob   What are you askin' that for?

Lizzie   I have to dae them for my hame lessons, and I canna dae them.

Bob   Decimals! Och, ay, they're easy.

Lizzie   Dae them for me, Bob.

Bob   You surely think it. I'm on strike, and I'm no' gaun to blackleg noo . . . By gee! I'm hungry.

Jenny (*to* **Bob**)   What's a' the noise aboot the nicht?

Bob   D'ye mean to tell me you dinna ken that there's likely to be a break-awa' the morn?

Jenny   Is there?

Bob   Ay, and that sweethe'rt o' yours is yin that would like to start . . . By gee! If he tries to go to the pit . . .

Jenny   Wha telt you that?

Bob   Never you mind, but it's true. Some man, him! My Uncle Tam is anither yin.

A shout is heard in the distance.

Listen! . . . that's anither meetin' in the fitba park.

He goes to fire and puts the poker up his sleeve.

Jenny   Where are you gaun wi' that poker?

Bob   I'll be yin o' the pickets.

Jenny   Put that poker doon and no' be daft.

She struggles with him and takes the poker from him.

If the polis catch you wi' that you'd get penal servitude. You stay here and leave the picketin' to the men.

Bob   Am I no' a man?

Lizzie   Some man.

Bob   I don't want ony o' your auld buck, see!

Jenny   And I don't want ony o' yours. Awa' doon and meet my mither.

Bob   I'm on strike

Enter **Kate**, *a dark, handsome lass, with a proud air.*

Lizzie   Can you dae decimals, Kate?

Jenny   No, she canna dae decimals.

Kate   I used to could dae them, Lizzie, I'll ha'e a try before I go oot . . . I'm up to see if you're gaun to the dance, Jenny?

Jenny   Your mither was sayin' you were gaun.

Kate   Too true I am.

Jenny   Where did you get the money?

Kate   Threepence for some auld jam jars . . . I think you should come, Jenny; it'll be a good dance.

Jenny   My shoon wouldna stand it, Kate . . . Are you in a hurry?

Kate   I'm finished hurryin', it's a mug's game.

Jenny   Tak' off your coat then, and sit doon.

She takes off her coat and hangs it over a chair. She sees **Bob**, *who is trying to light a stump of cigarette with a lighted paper.*

Kate   You're there, Bob? . . . No' thinkin' aboot startin' to your work?

Bob   D'ye see ony green in my eye?

Holds down his eyelash.

Kate   There's some thinkin' aboot startin', I hear.

Bob   Ay, and your faither's yin o' them.

Kate   Wha said that?

Bob   He said it himsel' at the street corner.

Kate   And did naebody bump him?

Bob   Tam Anderson telt him that if he tried it he would knock his bloody heid off.

Jenny   Here! Keep that kind o' language for the street corner.

Kate   I'll knock his bloody heid off mysel' if he tries it.

Bob   And the worm that rins efter Jenny here is talkin' aboot gaun to his work tae. By gee! Let him try it. I don't know where I'll be if he gets there without gettin' his skull cracked.

Kate   Wull Baxter! . . . Surely he's no' gaun to try and break awa', Jenny?

Jenny   He'll no' blackleg, Kate.

Bob   He was ay a gaffer's man, a belly-crawler.

Jenny   Shut up!

Bob   I ken him, Kate, for I worked beside him.

Kate (*to break conversation*)   Where's your faither, Jenny?

Jenny (*jerking her thumb towards room*)   Oh, lyin' in there wi' a fat heid . . . D'ye ken what he did yesterday?

Kate   No.

Jenny   He backed a double and came hame as drunk as a lord, singin' like a canary. And no' a crust in the hoose. He met in wi' some auld pal that's here on holiday frae America – so he says – and didna come oot the pub till the double was spent.

Kate   Was your mither wild?

Jenny   Wild! She was mad. I bet ye she put the singin' oot o' his heid.

Kate   Is your mither no' in?

Jenny   No, she's awa' looking for grub. That auld McIntyre the grocer wouldna gi'e her ony things this mornin'. 'I'll gi'e ye plenty,' says he, 'if you send your man back to his work.'

Kate   Eh! And what did she say to that?

Jenny   She spat in his face.

Kate   That's the stuff to gi'e them. I canna understand the tradesmen aboot here, they're a' up against the miners, but bad conditions for the miners means bad conditions for them, tae. They'll mebbe learn that some day when they're puttin' up their shutters . . . Let me see your sums, Lizzie.

Lizzie *goes to her with book and pencil.*

Bob   Don't dae them for her, Kate.

Lizzie   You mind your ain business.

Bob   I'll wallop your ear for ye if you set up ony auld gas to me. (*To* **Kate**.) She's as thick in the heid as a wudden leg. I wouldna dae them for her, I would let her get the strap.

Lizzie   You couldna dae them onywey. A' you can dae is play cairds and toss up pennies at the street corner – and swear.

Bob   Mind, I'll melt ye!

Jenny   That'll dae, noo, we a' ken hoo clever you are.

Bob   Would you like to hear a tune on my gramophone, Kate?

Kate   Ay, put it on, Bob, we're needin' something to cheer us up.

Jenny (*nodding towards the room*)   You'll wauken him.

Bob   What dae I care for him!

Puts the gramophone on the table and takes some records from the drawer in the dresser.

Kate   Here you are, Lizzie; I think that's richt.

Lizzie   I wish you had been my sister, Kate, Jenny's just a dunce.

Bob (*to Kate*)   By gee! You're a right mug, I would let her get the strap.

Lizzie *puts out her tongue at him as she packs her books in her bag.*

Bob   What d'ye want? 'Danny Boy'?

Kate   Oh, for God's sake, put on something cheery, and let Jenny and me get a dance.

Bob *starts the gramophone.* **Kate** *takes a hold of* **Jenny**, *and they begin to dance.* **Bob** *watches them for a time, then he grabs hold of* **Lizzie**. **Bob** *and* **Lizzie** *are footing it at the room door when it opens and* **Jock Smith**, *a typical miner, in his shirt and trousers and stockinged feet, enters. He brushes* **Bob** *and* **Lizzie** *aside in an irritated manner, and goes directly to water pail. He drinks greedily two 'tinnie' full. Then he makes for the fireside.*

Jock   Oh! Stop that damned thing!

Bob *jumps and puts the gramophone off.* **Kate** *winks at* **Jenny**.

Jock   What kind o' dance d'ye ca' that?

Kate   That's what you ca' the Charleston, John.

Jock   God kens what the world's comin' tae. Nae wonder you're a' knocked-kneed and in-taed gettin'.

Kate   What's in-taed?

Jock   The half o' ye are gaun aboot like a lot o' hens. (*To* **Jenny**, *curtly*)   Did you get a paper the nicht?

Jenny (*just as curtly*)   You're sittin' on it.

Jock *rises and gets paper under cushion.*

Jock (*opening paper*)   You're damned lucky that can think aboot dancin', that's what I have to say. (*Irritably.*) Where's the racin' page? . . . Ay, damned lucky that can think aboot dancin' . . . (*Looking at the race results.*) Weel, I'm damned if that's no hard lines.

Bob   It'll be a' the same to us.

Jock (*making a rush at him*)   I'll warm your ear for you, my lad.

Bob *scoots out.*

Lizzie   He's a cheeky devil that.

Jock (*to* **Jenny**)   Where's your mither?

Jenny   She's awa' seein' where she can get something to fill hungry bellies till we get some money frae the Pairish: awa' beggin', and lowerin' hersel' again. And there was nae need for it if you had played the game yesterday.

Jock   If the double had went doon what difference would it have made?

Jenny   But the double came up, and you gied the winnin's to the publican to help him buy anither motor car.

Jock   Hoo would you like to be me, Kate?

Kate   Onything fresh in the paper aboot the strike?

Jock   To hell wi' the strike. It should never have happened. I'm payin' nae mair Union money after this. I've got enough o' it this time. For thirty years I ha'e paid it, but never anither penny will they get frae me.

Kate   What?

Jock   Oor leaders. It's easy seen that this has a' been planned in Russia.

Kate (*with a smile*)   What makes you think that, Jock?

Jock   Look at the papers and you'll see pages aboot it every nicht. It's the Socialists to blame . . . I ken what they want, it's a revolution they want.

Kate   D'ye mean to tell me, Jock, that you've been locked oot for six months and doesna ken ony better than that?

Jock   It's you that doesna ken ony better . . . I was makin' a pound a shift before they broucht us oot on strike, Jenny there'll tell you that.

Kate   You must have been well in the know. My faither wasna makin' as much as feed a canary.

Jock   Twenty white shillin's a shift (*going to pail for another drink*) and the best o' conditions at that.

Kate   Are ye a Mason.

Jock   No, I'm no' a Mason.

Kate   It's a mystery to me.

Jock   God, but I'm dry . . . Make a drink o' tea, Jenny.

Jenny   The caddie's empty.

Jock (*drinks and returns to chair*)   No, this strike! strike! strike! idea'll no' dae.

Kate   But it couldna be helped.

Jock   Hoo could it no' be helped?

Kate   Weel, the maister wanted to reduce your wages and make you work langer 'oors, what else could you dae but strike?

Jock   We could have knuckled doon.

Kate   But you're a Scotsman, Jock.

Jock   I am, and prood o' it.

Kate   It doesna say much for Scotland.

Jock   No, of coorse, no', it says mair for Russia. I ken what I would dae if I was the Gover'ment. I'd get a boat and ship the hale damned lot to Russia.

Kate   Wha, the coalmaisters?

Jock   No, thae Socialists and Communionists.

Kate   But they didna reduce your wages?

Jock   I ken that fine.

Jenny   And if you ken that fine, what is the argument aboot?

Jock   What I'm sayin' is, that we'd been far better if we had knuckled doon. I kent we were gaun to be defeated.

Kate (*jumping*)   Wha said we were defeated?

Jock   I ken we are defeated.

Jenny   D'ye ken onything aboot backin' doubles and gi'en the winnin's to the publican?

Jock   Oh here! We've heard enough aboot that, give it a rest . . . Bring me a drink, Lizzie.

Lizzie   What kind o' drink, Daddy?

Jock   Ha'e some savy.

Lizzie *goes to pail.* **Wull Baxter** *enters.*

Wull   Hullo, Kate. And how's the health?

Kate   Not too bad, considerin' we're slowly fadin' away.

Wull   That's a fine nicht, John.

Jock   Is it?

He takes 'tinnie' from **Lizzie** *and drinks.*

Wull   You're lookin' rather wild like, John. What's wrang?

Jock   Oh, Kate and me have been ha'in' an argument.

Wull   Ay. What's the trouble?

Jock   The strike.

Wull   We're thinkin' gey seriously aboot it noo . . . We werena expectin' it to last as lang as this.

Jock   A piece o' damned nonsense and thrawness. I've been tellin' her that I've payed my last penny to the Union.

Wull   I'm finished wi' the Union tae.

Kate   What's that you say, Wull?

Wull   The Union has failed us, Kate. They ken damned fine the battle's lost long ago, and they should have cried the strike off.

Kate   We've naething to lose noo, and we may as well fight to a finish.

Wull   If we saw ony signs o' the finish it wouldna be sae bad. But it's likely to go on for months yet, if it's left to oor leaders.

Kate   Weel, let it go on. The coalmaisters'll mebbe no' be sae keen to lock us oot again.

Wull   We dinna ha'e a very guid case, either. We can see noo that the pits havena been payin'.

Kate   Havena been payin'! But has that no' ay been their cry? Was that no' their cry when the women worked doon the pits?

Wull   There wasna mony women worked doon the pits.

Jock   They were in the pits, Wull. My faither was born doon the pit.

Wull   Born doon the pit.

Jock   Ay, born doon the pit . . . It's no' everybody can bum aboot that.

Kate   Something to bum aboot: a woman workin' doon the pit till the very minute o' confinement . . . And still the pits didna pay.

Jock   Ay, my granny carried coal up the auld stair pit for mony a lang day. What's mair, she helped to lift the stane off my grandfaither when he was killed.

Wull   Is that true, Jock?

Jock   Helped to lift the stane off him; helped to cairry him hame a corpse . . . And you're grumblin', Kate, but you dinna ken you're alive. Frae daylicht to dark they had to work then; the only time they saw daylicht was on the Sunday.

Kate And still the pits didna pay.

Jock I ken that fine, you didna need to tell me that.

Kate And if the miners hadna foucht against it your women micht have been workin' in the pits yet.

Jock I ken that fine!

Kate They had to fight to make things easier for you.

Wull We're fightin' a losin' fight, Kate, you canna deny that.

Kate We are, if a' the men are like you. But they're no', and we're gaun to win yet.

Wull It's too late in the day to win noo. And the sooner it comes to an end the better for everybody concerned.

Kate Mebbe you're yin o' them aboot the place that wants to bring it to an end.

Wull I have been thinkin' aboot it, but I havena made up my mind yet.

Kate If you've been thinkin' aboot it, Wull, you've made up your mind.

Wull Weel, to tell you the truth, I didna see the use o' carryin' on much langer.

Kate Then you're no' the man I thocht you were.

Wull No?

Kate No, you are not. I never thocht you would stoop sae low as split on us.

Wull I'm no' splittin'. But when word comes that the Pairish Cooncil is no' payin' ony mair relief, it's time something was done to bring it to an end.

Kate No' payin' ony mair relief! Wha tellt you that?

They are all attentive.

Wull   The cooncil had a meetin' the noo, and that's their decision.

Kate   I've been expectin' it.

Jock   That'll put us in a nice mess.

Wull   It's as weel it has come to that, Jock, for it'll bring the issue to a heid. It'll end the strike here.

Kate   Starve the women and bairns to force the men back to their work. (*Rising and facing* **Wull**.) And you agree wi' that policy.

Wull   There's nae ither way that I see.

Kate   I have only yin answer for you, and it's *this*!

She hits **Wull** *a severe slap on the face.* **Wull** *staggers. They all rise excitedly.*

Jock   Kate!

Wull (*rushing at* **Kate**, *who stands her ground*)   You flamin' tinker! Ye . . .

Jock (*holding* **Wull** *back*)   Never heed her, man!

Jenny *goes to room crying.*

Kate   Keep your hands off me, ye blackleg . . .

Jock   Kate!

Kate (*to* **Wull**)   Ye traitor.

Bob *enters excitedly.*

Bob   That's it noo; nae Pairish money the morn, and a hunner polis in at the pit to smash up the pickets.

Kate (*with hysterical laugh*)   And Britons, never, *never* shall be slaves.

Bob   It's a revolution that's needed here.

Jock   See here! If I hear tell o' you gaun to ony mair o' thae Bolshie meetin's I'll scud your ear for ye.

Wull   I'll be in later, John, I want to ha'e a talk wi' ye.

Kate   Ay, awa' oot o' the sicht o' decent folk – ye scab!

Wull *would return to her, but* **Jock** *signs to him to go out.*

Bob   Was he sayin' he was gaun to his work in the mornin'. He has been in the office wi' the manager, and his mither has been getting' his pit buits mended at the store. By gee! If he goes to his work in the mornin' there'll be nothing left o' him but a big bubble.

Jock   Did you see your mither doon the street?

Bob   No, I've mair to think aboot than look for my mither . . . A flamin' worm like that . . .

Jock   Awa' and look for your mither!

Bob   He's worse than a worm, he's a dirty rotten blackleg.

Jock   D'ye no' hear me speakin' to ye!

Bob   If he goes to his work I'll flatten his face wi' a half brick.

Jock *rushes at him and he scoots out.*

Jock   Nae Pairish relief, Kate. Hoo dae they think we're gaun tae live?

Kate   It's murder, Jock. And the likes o' Wull Baxter, a workin' man, agreein' wi' it. I canna understand it. It's laughable.

Jock   Something to laugh at; no' a crust in the hoose the nicht, and nae hopes o' getting' ony the morn. Ach, I'm fed up wi' the hale blasted thing.

He goes to room.

Lizzie   Is that the strike finished noo, Kate?

Kate   No, it's no' finished hen, it's just startin'.

Lizzie   I wish it was finished till I get my new frock.

Jenny *enters.*

Kate   What d'ye think o' that, Jenny?

Jenny   I canna understand him, Kate, I didna think he was yin o' thae kind.

Kate   Neither did I. But dinna break your he'rt ower him, he's a guid riddance.

Jenny *sobs.*

Kate   Noo, noo, Jenny, dinna greet; thank your lucky stars you ha'e got rid o' him.

Jenny   We were to get mairrit when the strike was finished.

Kate   The dirty swine!

The door opens and **Tam Pettigrew** *enters, standing at the door.*

Tam (*to* **Kate**)   Are you gaun to stay here a' nicht?

Kate   What d'ye want?

Tam   Your mither's in her bed, and I want you to get my pit claes ready.

Kate   Your what?

Tam   My pit claes; I'm gaun oot to my work.

Kate   Oh, are ye! And are we to have nae say in this?

Tam   Wha?

Kate   My mither and me?

Tam   What the hell have you to do wi' it?

Kate   D'ye think I could walk through the streets o' Carhill again if you blackleg? D'ye think my mither could speak to the neebours again?

Tam   I'll soon be forgotten.

Kate   Blackleggin' is a thing that can never be forgotten.

Tam   But, Kate, we're in utter starvation, that's what has put your mither to her bed . . . And there's nae Pairish money the morn.

Kate   If you march a thousand strong to the Pairish offices they'll pay oot the money.

Tam   The polis are here to keep us frae marchin'.

Kate   It takes mair than polis to stop a hungry mob.

Tam   I'm gaun oot tae my work.

Kate   If you go to your work you'll come hame to an empty hoose. I'd rather tramp the country and beg my crust than stay in the same hoose as a blackleg.

Tam   But something has to be done, Kate.

Kate   Fight on to the finish, that's what can be done.

Enter **Jock**.

Jock   Did onybody see my pipe?

Lizzie   It's on the fender, Daddy.

She goes for it.

Jock   Weel, Tam!

Tam   Weel!

Jock   What are gaun to dae aboot it noo?

Tam   God knows.

Lizzie   You'll need to go back to the pit, Daddy.

Jock   The pit'll come to me before I go to the pit. I'll stay awa' frae it noo, just for spite. Stop the Pairish relief, what the hell'll be their game.

Kate   There'll be a riot here the morn if they try to stop it.

Jock   A lot o' guid that'll dae.

Tam   Ay, a lot o'guid that'll dae, Jock; half o' us clouted wi' a polisman's baton, and landed in the jile.

Kate   It's mair honourable to be clouted wi' a polisman's baton than clouted wi' a miner's fist, and that's what'll happen to the men wha try to blackleg.

Jock (*looking at pipe*)   No' a smoke either, Kate. It's a wash-oot!

Kate (*donning her coat*)   Keep up your pecker, Jock, there's a guid time comin' yet.

Jock   It's been comin' a' my time, but it's a damned sicht farther awa' noo than ever it's been.

Tam   Ay, a body would be better deid.

Kate   Did you ever hear such a crowd o' men? And they wonder why they're losin' the strike.

Tam   It's a' richt for you speakin', you havena the responsibility o' a hoose on your heid.

Jock   Ay, they're young, Tam, and doesna ken what it means to the likes o' us.

Kate   Puir sowls, without your baccy and your beer you're no' much use. (*To* **Jock**.) Stick oot your chest, man! Let them see you're a Scotsman and a man. Fight like hell, and never say die till a deid horse kicks ye.

Jock   It's no' easy for a hungry man to stick oot his chest.

Tam   It is not, Jock.

Kate   Well, stick your fingers to your nose at them. Guid nicht.

Jock   Guid nicht.

Kate *and* **Jenny** *go out.*

Jock   God kens what's to be done. For thirty years I have worked in the pit, and has come through many a hard time o't, but never the likes o' this.

Tam   I wouldna have troubled mysel sae much, but the wife's no' keeping weel ava: that cough o' hers is gettin' worse.

Jock   She'll need to take care o' hersel', Tam.

Tam   Tak' care o' hersel'! And hasna had a meal the day! I'll need to do something, Jock, I canna let things go on like this.

Jock   But what can you dae?

Tam   I can go to my work. It's the only thing I can dae.

Jock   It's a problem, Tam. I wish I could help ye, but I'm needin' help mysel'.

The sound of singing can be heard faintly. 'We'll hang every blackleg . . . '

Tam   Ach, to hell, I dinna ken what to dae.

He goes out.

Jock   Ay, it's a problem, Tam.

Lizzie   Will my mammie be long, Daddy? . . . Does she no' ken I'm hungry? . . . I wish the strike was finished, I'm needin' a new frock . . . See, I'm in rags . . . And I'm needin' shoon tae, my feet are ay wet.

Jock *is sitting gazing into the fire.*

Lizzie   My mammie was greetin' when I came hame frae the schule the day . . . Gimmie a piece, Daddy.

Enter **Jean**, *wearily, an empty basket in her hand. She is followed by* **Jenny**. **Lizzie** *runs to her mother, but* **Jean** *takes no notice of her. She puts the basket on the table, takes off her shawl, and sits down at table side, as if she was exhausted.*

Jock   Hoo did you get on, wife?

Jean   I'm beat, Jock, there's no' a grocer or baker in the toon'll gi'e me a crust.

Jock *(rising)*   Get oot my pit claes.

Jean *(rising)*   No, you're no' dain' that.

Jock What else can be done?

Jean You came oot wi' your neebours, and you'll go back wi' them.

Jock And have we to dee o' hunger?

Jean Something'll turn up yet.

Jock Oh! For God's sake ha'e some sense. What can turn up?

Jean *sits and breaks down.*

Jenny (*with her hand on* **Jean**'*s shoulder*) Ha'e ye nae he'rt! Barkin' at my mither like that when you ha'e mair need to be comfortin' her. For six months she has scraped through, and you've never kent what it was to want a bite or a smoke till the nicht; lowered hersel' mony a time to keep things gaun, and noo, when she's beat, you can only bark at her.

Jock I dinna mean it, Jean.

Jean I ken that, Jock, I'm no' worth a haet gettin'.

Jenny Mebbe my uncle, Bob, would help us?

Jean Supposin' we should dee you're no' gaun near him.

Jock Bob would help us if he kent we were in this hole.

Jean He's a blackleg, and we're no' askin' help frae him.

Jock Weel, something has to be done . . . Can we no' sell that gramophone?

Jean No, it's the laddie's.

Jock But something'll need to go, Jean?

Jean That gramophone's no' gaun. The laddie boucht it wi' the first pocket-money ever he earned; he'd break his he'rt if he were to lose it.

Jock Right-o! I'm gaun to the pit, for I'll starve for nae white man.

Jean (*rising and going to room*) You're gaun to drive me mad yet.

Lizzie *follows her mother.*

Jenny   For God's sake, Faither, ha'e some sense.

Jock   It's your mither that has nae sense. I'm shair that gramophone's no' needed at a time like this. And yet you'd starve rather than hurt his feelings. I canna understand it.

Jenny   If you were a woman you would understand it, you men ha'e nae he'rts.

Jock   It's past the time for silly sentiment. We're up against it, Jenny, and some o' us have to make a sacrifice.

Jenny   Weel, you should have sacrificed your beer yesterday. This wouldna have happened if you had played the game yesterday.

Jock   I ken that fine, you dinna need to tell me that, but it's past and canna be helped noo. Hoo are we gaun to get a crust o' breid, that's the question . . . Folk that ha'e toiled and battled a' their days, workin' frae hand to mooth, even in the best o' times, slaves, if ever there were slaves, and to think we've to go back to that pit on worse conditions! It's hellish to think o' it. It would be a God's blessin' if the roof came doon the first day and crushed the life oot o' us, they'd be responsible for oor wives and bairns, and we'd be awa' frae a' the bloody sufferin'.

Jenny   That's a selfish wey oot o' it, and it's selfishness and greed that's the cause o' a' the sorrow and sufferin' the day.

Lizzie *enters from room.*

Lizzie   Jenny, my ma wants ye.

Jenny *goes to room.* **Lizzie** *follows.* **Jock** *sits to put on his boots.* **Wull Baxter** *enters.*

Wull   Weel, that was some row the nicht, John . . . She's a right tartar, isn't she?

Jock   Ay, she has a temper.

Wull Ye ken, it's the women o' this place that's keepin' this strike gaun on.

Jock They seem to ha'e got their birz up.

Wull Hoo are things wi' you the nicht, John?

Jock No' too bad, we've been worse mony a time.

Wull The morn'll tell a tale when there's nae Pairish relief.

Jock It'll tell a tale someway or ither.

Wull I'm thinkin' aboot tryin' to get oot to Canada. There's naething here for a young chap.

Jock It's no' easy gettin' oot there.

Wull I'll manage . . . The men that are startin' the morn are gettin' a guid chance.

Jock Are they?

Wull Five pounds when they make a start and a pound a day.

Jock That's the stuff, eh!

Wull Isn't it. It's no' often the miner get a chance like that.

Jock No I can hardly believe it.

Wull You can take it frae me, Jock, it's the truth . . . What about it?

Jock What aboot what?

Wull Makin' a start in the mornin' wi the rest o' us?

Jock Eh! D'ye mean to tell me you're canvassin' for blacklegs?

Wull It's no' blackleggin'. You ken as weel as me that if it's left to the leaders it'll never be finished. The place is in ruination: if the pit doesna open soon it'll never open . . . A week's work would put you on your feet again.

Jock Would put wha on their feet?

Wull   Don't be silly, John, this chance only comes yince in a lifetime.

Jock   Wull, I'm hungry, richt enough, and money o' ony kind is a big temptation, but before I would touch their blood money I would eat grass at the roadside.

Wull   Are you feart for the Socialists and the pickets?

Jock   I don't want ony insults, Wull.

Jenny *makes to enter, but when she sees* **Wull** *she returns.*

Wull (*rising*)   I thought you had mair pluck than that, Jock.

Jock (*rising and gripping him*)   Ye flamin' twister! If ye insult me like that I'll choke the life oot o' ye.

Jenny *and* **Jean** *come to door.*

Wull   I thought the way you were speakin' . . .

Jock   Oot o' my sicht, ye traitor! (*Throws* **Wull** *from him.*) And if I ever see Jenny speakin' to ye again, I'll cut your tongue oot o' her heid.

Jean *returns to room.*

Jock   Oot o' that door, I say!

Wull *goes out.*

Jock   Blackleg! No, I'm damned sure though it was a hunner pounds a shift . . . Jenny, I came oot like a man and I'll go back like a man; it'll never be said that Jock Smith was a blackleg.

Enter **Bob**.

Bob   Was Wull Baxter in here?

Jock   Ay.

Bob   Was he wantin' you oot to your work?

Jock   Never you mind.

Bob   If you go to your work I'll leave the hoose.

Jock   Is there a meetin' the nicht?

Bob   There's a meetin' the noo to get pickets.

Jock   Awa' to the meetin' and let me ken what gangs on. I'll let you go this time.

Bob *is at door when* **Jock** *speaks.*

Jock   Bob! Come here a minute.

Bob *returns.*

Jock   We're up against it the nicht, Bob. Would you be vexed if we selt your gramophone.

Bob *is silent.*

Jock   We'll get you anither yin when the strike's finished.

Bob *is on the verge of tears.*

Jock   We're at oor wit's end. Your mither has been in every shop in the toon and canna get a crust without the money. And Wull Baxter was in here the noo offerin' me a pound a shift if I went to my work. I dinna want to go, Bob, but if we have to starve, weel.

Bob   You can sell it, Faither.

Jock   Your mither doesna want to pairt wi' it.

Bob   I'll tell her.

He goes to room.

Jenny   They've even to draw blood frae the he'rt o' the bairns.

Jock   I didna think I was sae sentimental.

Re-enters **Bob**.

Bob   It's a richt, Faither, I tellt her I was tired o' it. (*Going off.*) I ken what's needed, it's a revolution that's needed.

Jock   I'll need to get a breath o' fresh air, this nicht has me about suffocated.

He dons muffler and jacket. A knock comes to the door. **Jenny** *goes to answer.*

Jenny   It's Tam Anderson.

Jock   Come in, Tam!

Tam Anderson *enters and* **Jenny** *goes to room.*

Tam   Was Wull Baxter in here soundin' you aboot gaun to the pit this mornin'?

Jock   He was.

Tam   Are you gaun, Jock?

Jock   Am I hell!

Tam   Isn't he a richt traitor? Did you think he was yin o' thae kind?

Jock   No, or he'd been coortin' some ither place . . . D'ye think there'll be mony that'll try to go oot, Tam?

Tam   I couldna say. I heard Tam Pettigrew was thinkin' aboot it tae.

Jock   I dinna think Tam'll be there, though Tam's up against it the nicht . . . If the Pairish doesna pay ower the morn I doot there'll be a big breakawa'.

Tam   The Pairish'll pay ower, Jock, or we'll tear doon the buildin'. We're formin' pickets for the morn, Jock, will you gi'e us a hand?

Jock   I will, and if that Wull Baxter tried to pass me it'll be a face without a nose. Is there onything I can dae the nicht?

Tam   We're ha'in' a secret meetin' to discuss the plans for the morn, you can come if you like.

Jock *claps his hand. Then singing can be heard, the tune is 'The Red Flag'.*

Jock   That's the stuff to gi'e them! Blaw their blasted pits in the air, and the blacklegs wi' them (*As they go out.*) A pound a shift! No, I may sell my muscle; but I'll never sell my soul.

The singing fades away. **Lizzie** *enters.*

Lizzie   That's my daddie awa' oot, Ma!

Jenny *enters with her coat on. She lifts the gramophone and is near door when* **Jean** *enters.*

Jean   Jenny. We canna sell that gramophone yet. Tak' this ring instead.

She takes the ring from her finger.

Jenny   You canna sell that ring, Mither. Bob wouldna let you pairt wi' that.

Jean   I can pairt wi' it easier than the gramophone. Noo, Jenny, dinna argue aboot it. Hurry and bring up some groceries, you're a' hungry. Hurry, Jenny.

Jenny *goes out.* **Jean** *puts the kettle on the fire, then she sits.*

Lizzie (*after a pause*)   Maw!

Jean   What is it, dearie.

Lizzie   I'm sleepy.

Jean *takes her on her knee.* **Lizzie** *lays her head against her mother's breast. There is a short pause, then* **Jean** *speaks dreamily.*

Jean   We were a prood pair that day, Jock, a prood pair. Blue skies and sunshine and the birds singin' on every tree. But that was lang, lang syne . . . Nae struggle then, and nae tears, just sang and laughter. (*Sighs.*) Ay, changed days noo, Jock.

Lizzie *looks up in her mother's face. They kiss as the curtain falls.*

Act Two

The same as Act One. The following day, afternoon. The canary in the cage at the window sings merrily. **Jock** *sits at the fireside reading a racing paper.* **Jenny** *sits at the tableside, in centre of floor, trying to knock a few tackets in her shoes.*

Jock Canaries are like human bein's, Jenny, they canna sing when their stomachs are empty.

Jenny *makes no answer.* **Jock** *takes a stump of pencil from his pocket, wets it in his mouth and begins to write the names of the horses on a slip of paper which he takes from his pocket.*

Jock If thae three dinna make the bookie squeal the day I'll never look at a horse in the face again. (*Puts paper in his pocket, rises and goes to the window.*) I wonder wha it is that's workin' the day? I could bet you a thousand pounds it's that Wull Baxter. The dirty swine, if ever he comes aboot this hoose again, I'll swing for him.

Enter **Jean**.

Jean There's nae Pairish money the day yet.

Jock What! Are they no' payin' oot?

Jean No, there's a deputation awa' to Edinburgh, to see the Board o' Health, wha'ever he is. I thoucht your mairch to the Parish Council wouldna frighten them.

Jock Weel, I could have sworn they were gaun to pay oot, for they had the wind up properly.

Jean It was a' in the game, to get you awa' hame again. They ken fine that if they diddle you the first time you'll no' get the same crowd to mairch a second time.

Jock I believe you're richt, Jean.

Jean Did you ever see me wrang?

Jock We ha'e a lot to learn before we win a strike.

Jean   I hear them sayin' that Tam Anderson's likely to be arrested for the speech he made. What did he say?

Jock   He made a great speech, Jean. He had the blood boilin' in my veins. 'Fellow workers,' he says, 'are ye gaun to stand and see your wives and bairns starve to death before your e'en? Are you content to dae this and ca' yoursel's men? Fellow workers! We have been far ower meek in the past, the time has come when we've got to be prepared to let them see that we're prepared to die . . . '

Jean (*interrupting*)   Some hope.

Jock   D'ye think I wouldna shed my blood for you?

Jean   You'll no' shed your hair for me, let alane your blood.

Jock   Just wait till the time comes and I'll let you see . . . have you heard wha it is that's workin'?

Jean   Ay, its Wull Baxter.

Jock   I thoucht that. Hoo did he get through the pickets?

Jean   He was at his work before the pickets were oot o' their beds. Some pickets!

Jock   Weel, God pity him when he tried to get hame, he'll be torn frae limb to limb.

Jenny *rises and goes to room.*

Jean   Would you ha'e thoucht it o' him.

Jock   I ay had my suspicions o' him; he was too damned nice and too damned wise, beware o' thae kind every time.

Jean   If he had been a mairrit man wi' a family there would have been some excuse but he has naebody to keep but that auld tinker o' a mither o' his. He's made fine fool o' Jenny onyway.

Jock   She'll soon forget aboot him.

Jean   It's no' sae easy forgettin', Jock. They were to be mairrit after the strike, and she has been layin' by wee bits o' things for a while.

Jock   There's nae weddin' takin' place noo.

Jean   It's that mithe o' his that's to blame, she's been nagging at him to start to his work.

Jock   It's no' her to blame ava', he wants to make a wheen pounds and slip off to Canada, I saw that was in his mind last nicht when he was in here.

Jean   Jenny has been speakin' aboot Canada tae.

Jock   Ay, a fine thing that would be, a douchter o' mine gaun to Canada on blood money. Jean, if he ever comes aboot this hoose again I'll leave him deid on the floor.

Enter **Agnes**.

Jean   Hullo! Agnes, I thoucht you were in your bed?

Agnes   I canna lie, Jean.

Jean   Did you get a sleep last nicht?

Agnes (*hopelessly*) No.

Jock   You'll need to see the doctor, Agnes, you're lettin' it gang ower far.

Jean (*decisively*)   The doctor's comin' the day, Jock, I'm sendin' for him mysel', we're standin' nae mair o' this nonsense.

Agnes   But, Jean, what's the use o' sendin' . . .

Jean (*interrupting*)   He's comin', and that's a' that's aboot it. D'ye ken you're like a ghost?

Agnes   There's nae Pairish money the day.

Jean   No. God kens what we'll dae, Agnes.

Jock   I ken what I would dae, I would get the miners to mairch to London and blaw Parliament in the air.

Jean   And where'll we be by the time you get to London?

Agnes   I dinna ken what to do, Jean. I'm just aboot mad.

She begins to cry.

Jean   Wheesht! Agnes, I'll see if I can dae onything for ye.

Agnes   The weans are a' greetin' for something to eat, and I ha'e naething. God, but I'm weary. I just want to lie doon and dee.

She has a fit of coughing. **Jenny** *enters.*

Jean (*taking her kindly by the shoulders*)   Come doon wi' me, Agnes, and get to your bed. I'll see that you get something to tide ower till they pay oot the Pairish money.

Agnes (*holding her brow*)   I'm tired Jean . . . tired . . . tired . . . tired, but there's nae rest.

Jean   I'll see that you dae get rest, supposin' I should sit at your beside till you fa' asleep.

Agnes   It's no sleep, Jean, it's . . .

She has another fit of coughing and **Jean** *leads her out, shaking her head sadly at* **Jock** *as she goes.*

Jock   You better go for a doctor, Jenny, there's something gey far wrang wi' Agnes.

Jenny   It's hunger that's wrang. I don't believe she has tasted a bite for days.

Jock   It's hellish! And we can dae naething tae help, naething ava. And they wonder why we mairch in oor thousan's wavin' the red flag. If they could only suffer oor lot for a week they wouldna wonder sae much. And that Wull Baxter oot workin'! Cutting oor very throats.

Jenny   I didna ask him to gang, Faither.

Jock   I ken, Jenny, and I'm vexed for ye. But the first time I'll meet him I'll take it o' his hide, the traitor.

Jenny *dons her coat.*

Jock   Forget aboot him, Jenny.

Jenny   I canna understand him, it was the last thing in the world I was expectin'.

Jock   Ay, ay, but things'll come a' richt for you yet, lass.

Jenny   I was lookin' forward to happy days, but everything has a' gane crash and in the yin day.

Jock   There's naebody escapin' the strike, Jenny, we're a' getting' a blow o' some kind. But we're learnin' and some day we'll mebbe get oor ain back.

Jean *enters, followed by* **Lizzie**.

Jean (*to* **Jenny**)   Awa' and get the doctor, Jenny. And bring up a gill o' whuskey when you're doon; that woman'll need to get a sleep or she'll be deid in the mornin'. You'll get a bottle in that end drawer.

She takes money from her purse.

(*To* **Jock**.)   Thae weans are in utter starvation.

Jock   Can you help her, Jean?

Jean   I'll gi'e her the half o' what I ha'e, I can dae nae mair.

She gives **Jenny** *the money for the whisky.*

Jean (*to* **Jenny**)   If Dr Morrison's no' in, go for the ither yin; the sooner we ken what's what, the better.

Jenny *goes out.* **Jean** *begins to put food in the basket.*

Jean   God be thanked we ha'e oor health and strength.

Jock   If she could get a sleep she would be a' richt; though I dinna like that cough, Jean, it's something deeper than a cauld.

Jean   I dinna ken, but we'll need to watch her weel, or she'll no' last long.

Tam *enters.*

Tam   Is Jenny awa' for the doctor?

Jean   Ay, he'll no' likely be long till he's up, Tam. I'm puttin' something in this basket for the weans. When had you onything last?

Tam   Yesterday mornin'.

Jean   And Agnes?

Tam   I dinna ken . . . She's had naething the day.

Jean   And what wey did she no' come and tell me?

Tam   She's no' a guid moocher, Jean, she would dee before she would ask onything.

Jean   I'm sure she kens she needna ha'e ony fears o' comin here.

Tam   She's ay been queer that wey.

Jock (*to* **Tam**)   Was you in the mairch to the Pairish Council this mornin'?

Tam   No, I was not; you'll no' get me takin' pairt in any o' your Bolshie stunts.

Jock   No, but you'll take the Pairish money when it comes.

Tam   Ay, *when* it comes.

Jock   We'll never get it sittin' at the fireside or lyin' on the grass . . . Were you no' on the pickets this mornin' either?

Tam   No, I think mair o' my bed.

Jock   Ay, but strikes are no' won in bed.

Jean   Nor in the pub, either?

Tam (*to* **Jock**)   Was you on the picket?

Jock   Too true I was. Up at the pit at five o'clock.

Jean   He's been singin' 'The Red Flag' since he came hame.

Jock   This country's gaun to be a wee Russia if this strike lasts much longer.

Tam   And would you like to see it a wee Russia?

Jock   Yes! And the sooner the better.

Tam   You had ay plenty to say against the Bolshies and Russia before.

Jock   Ay, but my brains seem to be in my stomach.

Tam   Weel, I don't want to see this country made into a wee Russia, it would bring it to ruination.

Jock   Ruination! That's the worst o' havin' a three-course breakfast, it makes a man a hunner per cent Britisher.

Tam   If there's nae Pairish money the morn I'm gaun to work.

Jock   A man that's feart to mairch to the Pairish Council doesna ha'e the pluck to face the pickets. You'd been at your work this mornin' if you hadna been feart.

Tam   I ken, and so would anither hunner men in the place. It's the damned Bolshies that's keepin' us frae startin'.

Jock   And here's luck to them, says I.

Tam   And it's them that dinna want to work that's on the pickets.

Jock   D'ye mean that I dinna want to work?

Tam   I never mentioned you.

Jock   I was on the picket, and I'm damned sure I'll work beside you ony day.

Tam   Did I say you couldna?

Jock   No, and you better no'.

Jean   Yo look like a pair that'll dee wi' the shovel in your hand. (*To* **Tam**, *handing him the basket.*) Here! Take this doon, and look slippy.

Tam   Did I say he couldna work, Jean?

Jock   O' coorse you did.

Tam   I did naething o' the kind.

Jean   Did I tell you to look slippy?

Tam (*as he goes out*)   Oh, ay, take his pairt. (*He shuts the door rather loudly.*)

Jock   Isn't he an agitator? Ay talkin' aboot work, and has never worked a' his days; he has starved his wife off the face of the earth.

Jean   I've lost about ten stane mysel' since I got mairrit.

Jock   You're a delicate lookin' cratur.

Jean *pours out tea into a 'tinnie' and gives it to* **Lizzie** *with a piece of bread.* **Lizzie** *sits on fender.*

Jean   If it wasna for my guid nature I'd been a walkin' skeleton.

Jock (*putting on his coat*)   There's yin thing I admire aboot ye, Jean, and that's your pluck.

Jean   I'm glad you appreciate it.

Jock   I do, and I thank my lucky stars mony a time that I got the wife I did.

Jean   Weel, what's the use o' continually grumblin' and grousin'; it does nae guid.

Jock   Not a bit. D'ye ken, Jean, I'm prood o' ye.

Jean (*looking at him in surprise*)   Ay!

Jock   I am, as prood as Punch. (*Coughs.*) Can you spare eighteenpence for a three-cross double?

Jean   I kent there was something comin'. No, I can no'. I ha'e mair need o' eighteenpence than gi'ein' it to the bookie.

Jock   They're three solid pinches, Jean, I could stake my shirt that twa o' them'll win.

Jean   Weel, you can stake your shirt.

Jock   Can you no' spare ninepence then.

Jean   Ninepence gets a loaf, and there's a family doon there in starvation.

Jock   If it comes up I'll promise to gi'e ye every penny . . . If you don't speculate, Jean, you'll never accumulate . . . if I don't win money wi' this line the day, I'll list up in the Salvation Army.

Jean (*taking coppers from her purse*)   Oh, here! There's a bob, you can get a glass o' beer wi' the extra threepence.

Jock (*taking the money*)   You're a sport, Jean.

Jean   Hook it! That's a' you're gettin'.

Jock *is on his way out when* **Bob** *enters, boisterously bumping into him.*

Jock   Here! Can you no' watch where you're gaun, ye muckle nowte!

Bob   It was you that wasna watchin' where you were gaun.

Jock   If you gi'e me ony o' your lip I'll slap your ear for ye.

Jean (*to* **Jock**)   Awa' you and attend to the bookie.

Jock   He's daft, that's what's wrang wi' him.

Jock *goes out.*

Jean (*to* **Bob**)   Where ha'e you been?

Bob   Washin' tatties at the soup kitchen. Is there onything for me to eat?

Jean   See here! You'll need to try to control your belly a bit, it would take a Carnegie to keep this hoose gaun the noo.

Bob   Eat when you can get it, and when you canna get it, weel, you canna eat.

Lizzie   I heard him swearin' the day, Maw.

Bob   Wha heard me swearin'?

Lizzie   Me.

Bob   You're a flamin' wee liar. Where did you hear me swearin'?

Lizzie   At the street corner.

Bob   What did I say.

Lizzie   You just want me tae swear tae, but I'm no'.

She puts out her tongue at him. He makes a rush at her.

Bob   I'll warm your ear for ye.

Jean   Here! That'll dae!

Bob   She's a flamin' wee liar.

Jean   That'll dae I'm sayin'!

Bob   Just wait till I get her outside, I'll bump her.

Jean   D'ye want ony tea?

Bob   Is there ony ham left?

Jean   No.

Bob   Never mind tea, then, just gi'e me a piece in my hand.

Jean *spreads bread with treacle.*

Bob   I'm fed up wi' this treacle, I'll soon be like a darkie.

Jean   Be damned thankfu' you're gettin' treacle. If the Pairish doesna pay oot you'll be doon on your knees on the grass.

Bob   Ha'e you heard the latest?

Jean   No, what is it?

Bob   Tam Anderson's coortin' Kate.

Jean   That's auld news.

Bob   Did you ken?

Jean   Surely I kent when it was me that gi'ed him the wink that she had a notion o' him.

Bob   Can you no' gi'e somebody the wink to tak' a notion o' me?

Jean   Wha would tak' a notion o' you?

Bob   What's wrang wi' me?

Jean   There's a lookin' glass there.

Enter **Jenny**.

Jean   Did you get the doctor?

Jenny   He's comin' doon after he gets his dinner.

She hands her mother the whisky.

Jean   You'll rin doon wi' this to your auntie's, Bob, and tell Kate that I'll come doon when the doctor comes.

Bob (*to* **Jenny**)   That Wull Baxter o' yours is gaun to get a maulin' when he comes up the pit; a' the women o' the place are gaun to be there; they'll skin him alive.

Jean (*to* **Bob**)   Tell Kate to make the half o' that into toddy, and gi'e it to her mither.

Bob   He's just a flamin' reactionary, but just wait till he gets a taste o' the dictatorship o' the proletariat.

Jean   Here! Chuck that Bolshie stuff and rin doon wi' that whisky.

Bob (*going off*)   There's nothing like direct action for the revolutionary movement.

He goes off.

Jean   I wouldna worry mysel' ower Wull Baxter, he's no' worth it.

Jenny   I'm no' worried, Mither, just disappointed.

Jean   Was he speakin' aboot gaun to Canada after the strike?

Jenny   We were baith gaun there.

Jean   That's the reason he's workin', Jenny.

Jenny   I canna understan' it, mither.

Jean   He'll get his desserts yet, Jenny, just bide your time. Every dog gets its day.

Jenny *looks out window wearily.*

Lizzie (*rising and handing her mug to* **Jean**)   Read my cup, Maw.

Jean *takes mug and looks into it with a serious air,* **Lizzie** *is serious too.*

Jean   There's a new frock comin' to you, dearie . . . but I doot it'll no' be till the strike's finished.

Lizzie   Nae stockings?

Jean   Ay, there's stockin's and shoon tae.

Lizzie   Nae money?

Jean   No, there's nae money, daurlin'.

Lizzie   And hoo will I get a new frock, and shoon, and stockings without money?

Jean   Rin awa' for a pail o' water, darlin', and I'll mebbe be able to tell you when you come back.

Lizzie *goes for pail.*

Lizzie (*going out*) This should be Bob's work, no' mine. Nae wonder I'm getting grey-heided.

The canary sings.

Jean   I wish I'd been a bird.

Kate *enters.*

Kate   Is Jock in, Auntie?

Jean   No. What d'ye want wi' him, Kate?

Kate   Will there be ony chance o' me gettin' some money if I go to the Pairish Clerk? I'll need to get some nourishment for my mither . . . she's beginnin' to rave noo . . . Oh Jean! I dinna ken what to dae.

Jean   Where's your faither?

Kate   He's sittin' at her bedside.

Jean   It's him that'll need to go to the Pairish, Kate, they'll no' listen to you.

Kate   He'll no' gang.

Jean   He'll gang if I go doon to him, and in a hurry.

Enter **Lizzie** *with water.*

Jean   Is her cough ony better yet?

Kate   Ay, she's no' coughin' noo, just ravin' aboot the weans.

Jean   The doctor'll gi'e her a bottle that'll make her sleep, and she'll be like a new woman in the mornin'. She's been worryin' hersel' ower much, that's a' that's wrang wi' her. You should have had the doctor lang syne, Kate. But that's what's wrang wi' the working women, they want tae dee on their feet . . . Tam Anderson would tell you what was the best thing to do to get some money frae the Pairish.

Kate   I hear them sayin' that he's likely to be arrested if he takes pairt in the demonstration against Wull Baxter.

Jean   If I see him, Kate, I'll ha'e a talk wi' him aboot it. He canna afford to take the risk o' gettin' the jile noo when the strike's aboot finished.

Kate   If he has his mind made up, Jean, you'll no' put him off it . . . Everything seems to be gaun wrang tigither . . . I'm fed up.

She buries her head in her hands at table and sobs.

Jean (*comforting*)   It'll no' dae to lose he'rt, Kate. When things go against us we've still got to battle. Lyin' doon to things doesna help ony. Na, na, let us keep oor he'rts . . . Wheesht! Lass things'll come a' richt for us yet. Awa' doon to the hoose and get your faither to go to the Pairish Clerk; if he doesna get onything I'll go for Tam Anderson and see what he has to say aboot it. Go doon and attend to your mither, gi'e her the rest o' the toddie till the doctor comes, then I'll come doon and see what's trumph.

Kate *rises.*

Jean   That's the spirit, hen, keep up your pecker . . . Go doon wi' her, Jenny, and keep her company till the doctor comes . . . Your mither will be a'richt the morn', Kate, dinna worry aboot that.

Kate *and* **Jenny** *go out.*

Jean   Puir sowl, she hasna had much pleasure in life to be a young lass.

Lizzie   What's wrang wi' my auntie, maw?

Jean   Hunger, dear, that's what's wrang.

Lizzie   What wey are folk hungry?

Jean   Because some are ower fu' fed.

Tam Anderson *knocks and enters.*

Jean   Did you meet Kate and Jenny, Tam?

Tam   I dinna want to meet them, Jean.

Jean   She's lookin' for you.

Tam   Is her mither nae better?

Jean   She's wantin' to ken hoo she'll get some money frae the Pairish Clerk; they're in utter starvation.

Tam   If she gets a line frae the doctor I'll see that she gets something. Tell her that, will ye?

Jean   What wey dae you no' want tae see her?

Tam   I'm likely to be arrested the nicht, Jean.

Jean   Hoo d'ye ken?

Tam   The sergeant o' the police warned me that if I took pairt in the demonstration against Wull Baxter I'd be arrested.

Jean   And are ye?

Tam   If we let him get hame withoot a demonstation there'll be mair men oot the morn. We've got to nip it in the bud, Jean.

Jean   Is it worth it, Tam? It means the jile for ye, and the breakawa'll take place some time or ither. You nor onybody else can stem it, and you ken that, for it has happened before in your time.

Tam   And it'll happen again, Jean, and will happen till the workers control their ain destiny. But we've got to fight till the last ditch every time, whether it means the jile or no'.

Jean   It'll hurt Kate, Tam.

Tam   I ken it will, but there's nae escape. I'll no' likely get ony mair than three months, and it'll be worth the sufferin' to come back again and ken that I did my bit.

Jean   And you'll get a' your thanks for it in the yin day. The miners are a queer crowd, they forget about the fight when they get their first week's pay in their hand. You ken the trouble you had after the last strike collectin' money to pay the debts you had to pawn your ain watch to help.

Tam   I ken a' that, Jean, but it has a' to be suffered, there's never onything won withoot a struggle . . . but I didna come up to argue wi' ye, Jean, I want you to take a message to Kate. I'm no' likely to see her for a while noo.

Jean   What d'ye want?

Tam   Will you ask her to stick to me, Jean?

Jean   You needna ha'e fear o' that, Tam. But would you no' be better to ha'e a talk wi' her yoursel'?

Tam   I'm feart she micht put me aff takin' pairt in the demonstration, you ken what women are, and she micht keep me back; at least we micht quarrel aboot it, and I dinna want that to happen . . . Tell her, Jean, that whenever I get oot we'll get mairrit . . . and Jean, I want you to gi'e her this; it'll mebbe tide them ower the strike.

Jean   What is it?

Tam (*holding out his hand*)   Three pounds, a' I ha'e left o' my savin's. It's no' much, but it'll ay help a wee thing. I'll no' need it, I'll be getting' free digs where I go. (*He smiles.*)

Jean   I wish you would put this affair off, Tam. No, I dinna wish it either, laddie, for if you did you wouldna be Tam Anderson. But, Tam, you'll no' dae very weel in the jile, you're no' the jilebird type.

Tam   If my health doesna break doon, Jean, I dinna care, but this strike has been a tryin' time, and my nerves are a' knocked to bits. But never mind, auld yin, we'll come through it. You'll keep Kate's he'rt up till I come back?

Jean   She'll be waitin' on ye comin' back, Tam, ha'e nae fear o' that.

Tam   Weel . . . Guid-bye, Jean.

He holds out his hand.

Jean   Guid-bye, Tam . . . This strike's gaun to break a' oor he'rts. (*She sobs.*)

Tam *wants to say more, but is not able. He goes out rather suddenly.* **Jean** *sits at tableside.* **Bob** *enters.*

Bob   By gee, there's gaun to be some fun when that worm Baxter comes up the pit; a' the women o' the place are getting ready for him. They're no' half wild because there's nae Pairish money the day. And the polis are comin' in their hunners.

Jean   You'll keep awa' frae it.

Bob   You surely think it! I'm gaun to be in at the death.

Jean   You're keepin' awa' frae it, I'm sayin' – and leavin' it to the men.

Bob   Leave it to the *men*! What am I?

Lizzie   A mug.

Bob   I'm no' gaun to warn you again.

Lizzie   You're worse than a mug, you're a . . .

Bob   A what?

Jean   That'll dae, the pair o' ye.

Bob   What am I?

Jean (*angrily*)   That'll dae, I'm sayin'!

Lizzie (*running out*)   You're a puddin'.

Bob *chases her the length of door.*

Bob   I'm wantin' a lend o' that poker.

Jean   What for?

Bob   A man's nae guid wi' his bare fists against a polisman wi' a baton.

Jean   Your faither'll be gaun, and that's plenty oot o' the yin hoose. I dinna want two o' ye to get the jile.

Bob   The jile! Will we get the jile?

Jean   Certainly you will.

Bob   I didna ken that. Will I get anither piece?

Jean   You'll get your tea at teatime.

Bob   By gee! When this strike's finished I bet ye I'll have yin solid tightener, I'll no' be able to eat onything for a week efter it. What about tuppence for a packet o' Woodbines?

Jean   I dinna ha'e tuppence; you're smokin' ower much onyway.

Bob (*going out*)   I ken what's needed, it's a revolution that's needed.

Jean *goes to cage and gives the bird some seed. Then* **Jock** *bursts in.*

Jock   That's twa o' my horses up, Jean! Thirty-five bob.

He catches hold of her and swings her round the room.

Jean   Thirty-five bob!

Jock   Thirty-five bob! And, if the ither horse comes up, you'll ha'e twa pound ten.

Jean   When will you ken aboot it?

Jock   No' till the mornin', but the thirty-five bob is as safe as the bank.

Jean   You'll see and come hame wi' it, Jock, and no' dae as you did the last time.

Jock   I'm safe enough noo, Jean, I got a lesson last nicht I'll no' forget in a hurry. (*Sits and lights pipe.*) A bit win like that fairly lifts up a body's he'rt, doesn't it?

Jean   It tak's something to lift up oor he'rts nooadays. I had Tam Anderson in the noo; he's to be arrested if he tak's pairt in the demonstration.

Jock   So I heard doon the street. But Jean, if they arrest Tam Anderson there'll be a riot.

Jean   Mebbe! I ken the Carhill miners; they're gey feart o' their ain skins whiles.

Jock   That's right enough tae let them sit on their hunkers at the street corner and let the likes o' Tam Anderson risk everything for them.

Jean   Are you gaun to the demonstration?

Jock   There'll be plenty there without me. (*Then to break the conversation.*) We'll get oot your weddin' ring wi' the bookie's money.

Jean   Let it stay where it is, we ha'e mair need o' the money than a ring on the finger.

Jock   I wouldna care if the strike was finished, it's been a hell o' a time.

Jean   You're no' gaun to be much better if you've to go back to the pit on the maister's terms. It's been a hard time, richt enough, and mony a nicht I have lain doon wonderin' where oor breakfast was to come frae, but Jock, it's nae mair he'rt-rendin' than watchin' thae wheels turnin' every day, and never lookin' oot the windie but dreadin' to see some o' ye cairrit hame a corpse or maimed for life. There are plenty o' women never bother their heids, they have seen that much and come through that much, that they have got hardened to it. But I havena reached that stage yet, na, thae wheels are ay between me and the sun, throwin' their lang, black shadows on the doorstep. It's mebbe been a time o' want since the strike started, but it's been a time o' peace; I was ay sure o' you and Bob comin' hame at nichts; but there's nae such faith when the wheels are turnin'. But you men dinna think o' thae things, you'll likely laugh at us when we tell ye aboot it?

Jock   It's a fact, Jean, we put nae value on oor lives.

Jean   You talk aboot a weddin' ring! I would gi'e the very he'rt oot o' my breist if I thought it would keep ye awa' frae that hell.

Jock   I'll need to try and get you awa' frae the pits, Jean, but it'll no' be easy noo they ha'e us gey weel chained, and I doot there's naething else for us but the same auld grind. Seven months' rent on oor heids noo, and we're a' needin' buits and claes. Ach. Christ kens what it'll be like.

Jean   Ay, but keep up your pecker, Jock, there's a silver linin' to every cloud.

Jock   So it says in the school books.

Enter **Jenny**.

Jenny   Mither, that's the doctor here, and he's takin' my auntie awa' to the hospital.

Jean   The hospital! What's wrang?

Jenny   I dinna ken, she has to go through an operation.

Jean   Good God! It's surely gey serious.

Jock   Did the doctor no' say what was wrang?

Jenny   No, he wouldna tell us.

Jean (*putting on a shawl*)   Puir sowl, I thoucht there was something gey far wrang wi' her.

She goes out followed by **Jenny**.

Jock   Starvation! And they write to America to say that there's nae distress in the coalfields. Christians! I wonder what Christ would think o' them if he was here.

Bob *enters.*

Lizzie   I heard him swearin' the day, Daddy.

Bob   I'll warm your ear for you if you say that again.

Lizzie (*running out*)   So you were, I heard ye.

Bob *chases her to door.*

Bob   Where's my mither?

Jock   Awa' wi the lodger.

Bob   I could dai wi' something to eat.

Jock   Weel, get it yoursel', God knows where some o' ye get the appetites. Are ye ay hungry?

He goes to dresser and puts bread and margarine on the table.

Bob (*cutting bread*)   There's gaun to be some fun at the pit when Wull Baxter gets up. Are you gaun up?

Jock   What am I gaun to do there?

Bob   Feart you get the jile?

Jock   No, I'm no' feart I get the jile.

Bob   What wey are you no' gaun then?

He spreads margarine on bread.

Jock   Hey! That's butter and there's a strike on.

Bob   That's no' butter, that's margarine.

Jock   Weel, ca' cannie wi' it. If you want tea you'll need to put water in the teapot.

Bob (*going to fire to fill teapot*)   Fancy oor Jenny engaged to a worm like Wull Baxter. I'm ashamed to go doon the street.

Sits down and puts sugar in his cup.

Jock (*at third spoonful*)   Here! Ca' cannie wi' that sugar.

Bob   Don't get excited. Where did you say my mither was?

Jock   Your auntie has to go to the hospital.

Bob   Oh, what's wrang wi' her?

Jock   If you kent that you'd be as wise as me, wouldn't ye?

He lights his pipe.

Bob   My uncle, Tam, was up at the Pairish tryin' to get some money, but he dinna get it.

Jock   No.

Bob   No, the clerk tellt him he heard his yarn before. But he'll get it noo if the doctor says it.

Jock   Ay, he'll get it noo when it's mebbe ower late. (*There is a short pause.*) I ha'e twa horses up the day, Bob.

Bob   By gee! Your jam's fairly in the noo.

Jock   Thirty-five bob. And, if the ither comes in, I'll ha'e aboot three quid.

Bob   That's the stuff to gi'e them. If you had that every day you'd be rich, eh?

Jock   Ay, *if.* If the Lakes o' Killarney were in Hell you'd get a shillin' a gallon withoot any trouble.

Bob   Would ye?

Jock   Ay, if!

Bob   If what?

Jock   Thick heid! Did you no' hear me say that if the Lakes o' Killarney were in Hell you'd get a shillin' a gallon!

Bob   What for?

Jock   For the water, of coorse!

Bob   Oh, ay. *If!* (*Spreading margarine on bread.*) If you hadna went into the pub wi' the last bookie's money . . .

Jock (*interrupting*)   Ca' cannie wi' that margarine, I said?

Bob   I'm doin' that, sir, it's no guid onywey.

Jock   Be damned thankfu' you're gettin' it.

Bob   I'm no' grumblin'. (*Pause.*) Did you hear aboot Sam Lindsay?

Jock   What Sam Lindsay?

Bob   Sam Lindsay, the bookie.

Jock   No, what aboot him?

Bob   He was pinched on the street the noo.

Jock (*jumping*)   Eh!

Bob   The polis pinched takin' bets on the street.

Jock (*almost in tears*)   I had my bet on wi' him.

Bob   Weel, you can say ta ta! to your money, the polis took a' the slips off him.

Jock   Cripes! That's a blow. Here! Ca' canny wi' that breid, are you aware that's a' we ha'e in the hoose?

Bob   Listen! That's them singin' 'The Red Flag'. By gee! There's gaun to be some fun here the day! It'll be anither Waterloo! Can *you* sing 'The Red Flag' yet?

Jock   Oh, shut up! It's bad enough backin' losers, but it's a damned sicht worse backin' winners, and no' gettin' paid ower.

Bob   I ay tellt ye it was a mug's game.

Jock   Shut up! I tell ye! And get thae things off the table. I thought Sam Lindsay had mair savvy than get pinched on the street. If I'd only put my bet on wi' Peter.

Bob   Ay, *if*!

Jock   I want less gab frae you, see! But if there's nae Pairish money the morn that gramophone o' yours'll need to go to the pawn.

Bob   My mither'll ha'e a say in that.

Jock   Wha's boss in here, me or your mither?

Bob   My mither, of course.

Jean *enters; she is crying.* **Lizzie** *follows, much concerned.*

Jock   What's the maiter, Jean?

Jean *is too much upset to answer.*

Jock   What has happened?

Jean   Oh, Jock, she's deid!

Jock   Deid! Good Lord!

Jean   Oh, Jock, that's an awfu' sicht doon there; a' the wean greetin' like to break their wee he'rts, and Kate tearin' her hair and cryin' on her mither to speak.

Jock   Where's the faither?

Jean   He's awa' to the Pairish wi' the doctor's line. But it's ower late noo. Oh Jock, she's worn awa' tae nothing, lyin' yonder wi' her thin white face.

Jock   Is there onythin' I can dae, Jean?

Jean   Naething ava', Jock.

Jock   Christ knows what it's comin' tae.

Jean   Puir wee things, they'll miss their mither. Gi'ed the bite oot o' her ain mooth, puir sowl. What can God be thinkin' aboot when He lets the like o' this happen.

Jock   If it's God's will that has ta'en awa' puir Agnes He's a gey queer God, and doesna' ha'e much o' a he'rt for the weans it seems.

Jean *rises.*

Jean   Fill the kettle, Jock, I'll need to go doon beside them the nicht. I'll leave Jenny wi' them the morn's nicht.

Jock   Right-o!

Jean (*going out*)   Puir wee things . . .

She goes out, **Lizzie** *following.* **Jock,** *fills the kettle with the water, spilling some on the floor. He puts the kettle on the fire then goes to scullery, returning with a cloth. He wipes the floor awkwardly and carries cloth away, as if it were a dead rat, by the tail, letting it drop on the way and has to clean up another mess. He chucks cloth through scullery door. He then lifts floor brush and sweeps the floor, making the best of a bad job. He puts table nearer the window to hide the mess. Then he sits at fireside. Through the silence the booing of a crowd can be heard at intervals. He goes to window and looks out.* **Bob** *enters excitedly.*

Bob   That's Wull Baxter up the pit, and he's comin' hame between twa regiments o' polis!

Jock   Are there mony women there?

Bob   Hunners, did you no' hear them booin'?

Jock   Could they not stay in their hooses and leave it to the men?

Bob   Leave it to the men! There's mair fecht in twa women than there is in a hunner men.

The booing is heard again.

Listen! Are you comin' to see the fun?

Jock   I ha'e mair to think aboot.

Bob   You're feart you get the jile, I'm no'.

He runs out. **Jock** *peers through window. The sound of disorder gets louder. There is one loud 'Boo!' then* **Jenny** *bursts in.*

Jenny   Oh, Faither, there's a riot started doon the street!

Jock   I kent it would happen. Could thae blasted women no' kept to their hooses onyway. (*Draws aside curtains of window.*) God Almighty! There's the crowd has got Wull Baxter awa' frae the polis! They'll lynch him . . . Jenny! Shut that door, he's making for here.

Jenny *stands undecided.* **Jock** *makes to lock door.* **Jenny** *holds him back.*

Jock   Oot o' my road, woman!

Jenny *struggles.* **Jock** *loses his temper, and thrusts her aside as the door bursts open and* **Wull Baxter** *almost falls in, locking the door behind him. The mob is at his heels, shouting madly. A stone crashes through the window.*

Jock   Oot o' this hoose!

Wull   They'll kill me, Jock!

Jock   Oot o' here, you traitor!

Jock *makes to eject him when the sound of a police whistle is heard and the screaming of women. Then a stampede, then silence.*

Jock (*at window*)   Bloodshed! Bloodshed ower the heid o' you! Oot o' here before I crush the life oot o' ye!

Wull *looks piteously at* **Jenny**. *She hesitates a second, then she goes to door, unlocks it, opens it. He goes out and she shuts the door again.*

Jock   Bloodshed ower the heid o' a worm like that! A traitor! A bloody skunk. And you would . . .

Jenny (*burying her head in her hands against the door*)   Oh! Faither!

He looks at her sympathetically as the curtain falls.

Act Three

The same as Acts One and Two. A week later. At rise of curtain, **Bob** *sits at tableside with a soup bowl on his knees, playing on it with two spoons as he would a kettle drum; he whistles a bagpipe tune.* **Jock** *enters from room, jacket off.*

Jock Is it no' time you were awa' to the soup kitchen?

Bob I'm waitin' till the last the day, it's aboot time noo I was getting' some o' the thick stuff.

Jock Ay, wait till the last, and, when you get doon, there'll be nane left.

Bob That'll be *my* funeral.

Jock Ay, but you'll be guzzlin' the dinner in here.

Bob Some hope when *you're* there.

Jock I don't want ony lip, see!

Bob *rattles on the bowl and whistles.*

Jock Oh, for God's sake stop that, it gets on my nerves.

Bob I think I'll join the pipe band.

Has another rattle.

Jock You'll break that flamin' bowl.

Bob No fear, sir.

Rattles still.

Jock (*rising*) Are you gaun to stop it?

Bob *stops.*

Bob It's high time we had the dictatorship o' the proletariat here.

Jock Did you hear ony word o' Tam Anderson when you were doon the street?

Bob   There's word comin' ower the telephone whenever the trial's finished.

Jock (*half to himself*)   I wonder hoo he'll get on?

Bob   Ten bob, or thirty days.

Jock   They're no' tryin' him in the High Court before a jury o' auld farmers and grocers and butchers to let him aff wi' a fine. I wouldna be surprised if he gets six months.

Bob   Away and don't haver! Six months! You're a reactionary. What would he get six months for?

Jock   If you had seen the summons you wouldna say that; they're just aboot chairgin' him wi' startin' a rebellion.

Bob   But it was Wull Baxter that was the cause o' it, no' Tam Anderson.

Jock   Ay, but Wull Baxter was helpin' the maisters, he was dain' richt as far as they were concerned.

Bob   But the maisters are no' tryin' him.

Jock   Are they no'? You ha'e a lot to learn aboot your revolutionary movement.

Bob   I ken mair than you ken; it's a revolution that's needed, and you dinna ken that.

Jock   I ken that when the revolution comes you'll be fillin' your belly some place.

Bob   When the revolution comes, sir, I'll be in the thick o' the dictatorship o' the . . .

Jock   Oh! Shut it!

Jean *enters carrying a basin containing potatoes, which she puts on the table and begins to pare.*

Jean   Is it no' time you were awa' to the soup kitchen, Bob?

Bob   I'm waiting on the thick stuff the day.

Jean   Ay, and you'll likely wait till it's finished.

Jock   I've just been tellin' him that, but you may as weel speak to the Bass Rock noo as speak to him.

Bob   I dinna ken what you're a' worryin' yoursel's aboot. If I dinna get ony soup it'll be me that'll be hungry, no' you.

Jock   I dinna want ony backchat, see!

Bob (*rising*)   If there's nae soup left for me there'll be a revolution doon there.

Jock   Revolution! And if onybody was burstin' a paper bag at your back you'd dee wi' the fright.

Bob   Oh, you're just a reactionary. When the revolution comes you'll be usin' propaganda for the bourgois. (*Going out door.*) Three cheers for the dictatorship o' the . . .

Jock *rises in a hurry, and* **Bob** *scoots.*

Jock   They damned Bolshies are settin' the young yins off their heids.

Jean   He's only a laddie, man. You're worse than him that pays ony attention.

Jock   Dictatorship o' the proletariat! And if you asked him what it meant, he couldna tell ye.

Jean   Do you ken what it means?

Jock   Ay.

Jean   What?

Jock   It means . . . it means . . . Weel, it means if . . . It means a revolution, that's what it means.

Jean   Ay, you ha'e a lot to learn yet tae, I doot . . . Hood'ye think Tam Anderson'll get on the day?

Jock   Six months!

Jean   Six months! He'll no' get off as easy as that.

Jock   Then, if you ken, what are you askin' for?

Jean   Just for fun. They're sayin' doon the street that they'll no' be ower hard on him seein' that the strike's aboot finished. But there's no' much sympathy wi' lawyers and judges, it's hard facts wi' them a' the time, hard, cauld facts; staring you through and through wi' their cauld, grey e'en seein' a' the bad points, but very few o' the guid yins.

Jock   It's true, Jean. Mebbe eichteen months for him, and the strike likely to be finished the day; it's hard lines . . . Ay, it's bad when you think aboot it, oot for seven lang months, hungered and starved just aboot off the face o' the earth, and to go back defeated.

Jean   Ach! You men dinna ken hoo to strike onywey; you throw doon your tools, come oot the pit, and stand at the street corner till you starve yoursel's back to the pit again. And when you *dae* go back, instead o' strikin' oot for mair on your rate, you fill mair hutches, and would cut each ither's throat to get them.

Jock   I ken there's a good wheen o' thae kind.

Jean   You're yin o' thae kind yoursel'. And you're grousin' aboot the langer 'oors you'll need to work, but you'll be awa' to the pit an 'oor before the time, and be an 'oor later in comin' hame frae it. Ach! you dinna ken the first thing aboot strikin', for as often as you've been on strike.

Jock   D'ye want us to blaw the pits in the air, or what?

Jean   If you'd slip oot the road and play cricket, and leave it to the women, you'd dae mair guid.

Jock   You ha'e plenty o' gab, if that would win a strike. I was at yin women's meetin', and I couldna hear a word for a week efter it, gab-gab-gab!

Jean   We ha'e mair than gab, we ha'e courage, and that's what you men dinna ha'e.

Jock   I'll bet you the next strike'll no' be sae quiet.

Jean (*sarcastically*)   The next strike! And you'll be breakin' your necks rinnin' up to the pit to get your jobs before the strike's finished.

Jock   What else can we dae?

Jean   Huh! I telt ye. Some men to win a strike.

Jock   The men were richt enough, it was the leaders that let us doon.

Jean   And wha puts the leaders there? Hoo often dae ye attend the Union meetin's? You tak' nae interest in your affairs till there's a strike on, then you find oot that you want new leaders. You just get the leaders you deserve.

Jock   There's a lot no' interested, right enough; of coorse it's a' for the want o' sense.

Jean   It's the want o' sense that makes a man buy that paper you're readin', tae, after a' it has said aboot ye since the strike started.

Jock   Eh!

Jean   That's a coalmaisters' paper you're readin'.

Jock   I ken that fine, you dinna need to tell me that.

Jean   Then what dae you buy it for?

Jock   Oh, just for the sake o' the pictures.

Jean   You'd be as weel to stop it, then, and buy *Comic Cuts*.

Jock   Where's Jenny?

Jean   She's doon at the soup kitchen, gi'en them a hand.

Jock   They tell me they're on their last bag o' tatties.

Jean   Ay, and as mony tattie pits aboot the place. It doesna say much for you men.

Jock   I think you want to see us in the jile.

Jean   The jile! You'd rather lie doon on a tattie pit and dee wi' an empty belly than risk the jile. I canna understand you men.

Jock   Where did you get *thae* tatties?

Jean   When you were studyin' the form o' the horses.

Jock   Wull Baxter was doon the street yesterday, I hear.

Jean   Ay, he was in the toon, at the shippin' office.

Jock   Gaun off to Canada likely?

Jean   Ay.

Jock   Does Jenny ken?

Jean   He sent a letter to her yesterday.

Jock   Oh! Did he! And what was in it?

Jean   Wantin' her to go to Canada wi' him.

Jock   Well, I'll be damned! Did you ever hear sic' neck? What did he say?

Jean   He's vexed for everything that's happened. Says it was for Jenny's sake he blacklegged – wanted to get as much as take them awa' frae here.

Jock   If you dinna watch her she'll slip off wi' him, that's what you'll see.

Jean   I'm kind o' vexed for him tae, Jock.

Jock   I telt ye. See here, Jean, there's to be nae damned nonsense aboot this. Wull Baxter's gaun to Canada *himsel'*! What would the neebours say aboot a thing like this?

Jean   To hell wi' the neebours! They dinna concern me, Jock.

Jock   It's no' happenin', see!

Jean   Wha said it was happenin'? I just said I was vexed for him.

Jock   Ay, but you're fishin' to get roon' the saft side o' me. I see the game a' richt.

Jean   You'd think you were boss in here the way you're talkin'. The saft side o' *you*. You havena had ony drink this mornin', ha'e ye?

Jock   There's somethin' in the wind when you're beginnin' to pity him noo. Vexed for him! And Tam Anderson likely to get the jile ower the heid o' him.

Jean   He made a mistake, that was a'. And that tinker o' a mither o' his made him go.

Jock   Where's his letter?

Jean   She says she burnt it.

Jock   Then she has mair sense than you.

Jean   Ay, she tak's it off her faither.

Jenny *enters, almost in tears.*

Jenny   Ha'e you heard aboot Tam Anderson?

Jock   No, hoo did he get on?

Jenny   Oh faither, he's got three years.

Jock   Three years!

Jean   Three years! That canna be true, Jenny.

Jenny   Ay, it's true, Mither, he's awa' to the jile for three years.

Jock   Good God! That's cruel. Three years! As quiet a laddie as ever stepped in twa shoon.

Jean   This'll send Kate mad. Puir sowl, she's ha'in' her fill o' sorrow the noo. Does she ken, Jenny?

Jenny   No. Will you go doon and tell her, Faither?

Jock   Will I go doon, Jean?

Jean (*at window*)   Here she's comin'. You'd better go to the room, Jenny.

Jenny *goes to room.*

Jock   This is a bad job, Jean.

Jean   Oh, this strike's gaun to break a' oor he'rts before it's finished.

Kate *enters. She is very pale and worn-looking.*

Kate (*holding out her hand*)   Here, Jean.

Jean   What is it, Kate?

Kate   Some money.

Jean   What is that for?

Kate   Just a wee bit help, Jean.

Jean   I dinna want it, Kate, you ha'e mair need o' it than me.

Kate   I got the insurance money the day, Jean. Tak' it, noo, or I'll be angry.

Jean   I'll tak' it, Kate, but I'll pay it back when the strike's finished.

She takes the money.

Kate   Ha'e you seen my faither this mornin', Jock?

Jock   No' me, Kate.

Kate   He went oot after breakfast time, and he's no' hame yet. He cam' hame gey fu' yesterday.

Jock   So I suppose.

Kate   D'ye ken, Jean, I'm weary.

Jean   I'm sorry for you, Kate, but you'll no' need to lose he'rt.

Kate   Hoo d'ye think Tam'll get on the day, Jock?

Jock   I dinna ken, Kate, I don't think they'll be too hard on him.

Kate   Will he get off, d'ye think?

Jock   I doot he'll no' get off, Kate.

He looks at **Jean**, **Kate** *sees him.*

Kate   Is the word in?

Jock   I dinna ken, Kate, I havena' heard onything.

He hangs his head.

Kate   You *ha'e* got word. Tell me, Jock. Tell me, Jean. Oh!
For God's sake tell me!

Jock (*putting his hand on her shoulder*)   Kate . . . I ha'ena very
guid news for ye . . . You'll need to bear up . . . They ha'e him
awa' for . . . three years.

Kate (*in whisper*)   Three years! . . . Three years! . . . Oh Jock!

She buries her head on his shoulder.

Jean (*going to her*)   Kate, dearie.

Kate *cries bitterly.*

Jean   Puir lass, I'm sorry for ye.

Kate   Three years! Oh. Jean . . . Jean!

Jean   Come awa' doon wi' me, Kate. Puir Tam!

They go out, and **Jenny** *enters.*

Jock   Three years, and we live in a civilised country. If this is
civilisation put me in among the savages. You better go doon
and keep her company a wee while, Jenny.

Jenny (*in a hysterical kind of way*)   Three years? And the miners
are feart for revolution. *Ha*! ha! ha!

She goes out. **Jock** *takes his pipe from his pocket; it is empty. He looks
towards door, then hurries to the tea caddie on the mantleshelf. He fills
pipe with tea, and is seated, puffing merrily, when* **Jean** *enters.*

Jean   Puir lass, she's in an awfu' state.

Jock (*puffing*)   She's gettin' *her* share o' the strike, Jean.

Jean   God kens she is. And that faither o' hers awa' boozin', I suppose. You'll need to ha'e a word wi' him; that kind o' conduct'll no' dae at a time like this; he'll break that lass's he'rt.

Jock   He has ay been the same, a washoot: the least excuse and off on the beer. He had the best wife in the country, tae, but dinna seem to ken it.

Jean   He'll ken noo, when she's awa'.

Jock   I'll ha'e to talk wi' him and see if I canna put some sense into his fat heid. (*Puffs.*) What ha'e you for the dinner the day?

Jean   Tatties and onions.

Jock   Stovies?

Jean   Ay. (*Coughs.*) What kind o' baccy is that you're smokin'?

Jock   Eh! It's . . . it's some 'ag ends I got frae Bob.

Jean   It's surely that, that's an awfu' smell.

Bob *enters carrying his bowl, which he puts on table.*

Jean   Hullo! Did you no' get your soup?

Bob   I was ower late.

Jock   I tellt ye, didn't I?

Bob (*to* **Jean**)   Ha'e you ony dinner, Mither?

Jean   Stovies and onions.

Bob   Some feed!

Jean   It's better than nane.

Bob   No' much . . . Is it true that the strike's aboot finished?

Jean   Ay, ham and eggs every Sunday mornin' noo.

Bob   If we had eggs, we could ha'e ham and eggs the noo, if we had ham.

Jock   Eh?

Bob   I'm sayin', if we had eggs, we could ha'e ham and eggs.

Jock   What the flames are you talkin' aboot?

Bob (*snuffing*)   What kind o' baccy is that you're smokin'?

Jock   What was wrang, there was nae soup?

Bob   Nae money left in the funds.

Jean   Did you hear aboot Tam Anderson, Bob?

Bob   No, hoo did he get on?

Jean   Three years.

Bob   Three years! I ken what's needed, it's a revolution that's needed.

Jock   Oh for God's sake gi'e that revolution a rest.

Bob   What kind o' baccy is that you're smokin'?

Jean (*coughing*)   It's fag ends.

Bob (*jumping*)   Where did you get them?

Jock   Never you mind.

Bob   I havena had a smoke the day. By Gee! When the strike's finished I'll smoke till I'm sick.

Jean (*putting on shawl*)   I'm gaun doon for something to eat. (*Lifting basket.*) Lift off that pot, Jock, you're bound to be tired o' stovies. We'll ha'e ham and eggs the day, supposin' we should never ha'e them again.

She goes out.

Bob (*shouting after her*)   Bring me a packet o' Woodbines, Mither. Ay, if we had eggs, we could ha'e ham and eggs the noo . . .

Jock (*interrupting*)   Oh! shut up.

Bob   Where did you get the fag ends?

Jock   I forgot to tell your mither I was needin' baccy.

Bob   She'll mebbe forget the ham and eggs, but she'll no' forget your baccy.

Jock   You better rin efter her and tell her.

Bob   She'll mind richt enough.

Jock   It's high time the wheels *were* gaun roond; wheen o' ye'll soon no' be able to walk wi' laziness.

Bob   I'm tired.

Jock   What dain'?

Bob   Rinnin' back and forrit to that soup kitchen on an empty belly. (*Suddenly.*) I wonder if she'll mind my Woodbines?

He jumps and rushes off. **Jock** *watches him go and shakes his head. He sits repeating, 'If we had eggs, we could ha'e ham and eggs the noo, if we had ham,' in a baffled way. He gives up. Then he lifts pot from fire and takes it to room.* **Lizzie** *enters from school. She takes off her schoolbag, then looks into the cupboard of dresser.* **Jock** *enters.*

Jock   What are you lookin' in there for?

Lizzie *is startled.*

Lizzie   I want a piece, Daddy.

Jock   You'll need to wait till your mither comes hame.

Lizzie   Where is she?

Jock   Awa' for ham and eggs.

Lizzie   Ham and eggs!

Jock   Ay, if we had eggs we could ha'e ham and eggs the noo . . . No, I'm damned if I can get that.

Lizzie   Eh.

Jock   Naething.

Lizzie   I couldna tak' my dinner at the schule the day, Daddy.

Jock   What was wrang wi' ye?

Lizzie   I got the strap frae the maister, and I was sick.

Jock   What did you get the strap for?

Lizzie   Because I dinna ha'e my hame-sums richt . . . See, Daddy.

She holds out her little hand.

Jock   Puir wee sowl, you had mair need o' guid diet the day than the strap. Ower fu' fed, and get their money ower easy, that's what's wrang wi' them. But I'll see him the morn, Lizzie, and he can tak' what he gets frae me, the dirty swine.

Lizzie   I ken what's needed, daddy, it's a revolution that's needed.

Bob *enters.*

Jock   Did you tell her aboot my tobacco?

Bob   No' me, she kens to get your baccy richt enough.

Jock   No, but you would tell her about your Woodbines?

Bob   That's what I ran efter her for. That's a fine state o' affairs doon there noo!

Jock   What's wrang?

Bob   Oh, they're flockin' up to the pit in their hunners to get their jobs back.

Jock   What are they dain' that for?

Bob   There's a notice up at the pit that every man has to go before the manager before he gets his job back.

Jock   What's the big idea?

Bob   Every man has to promise to chuck up the Union.

Jock   Oh! And if we *dinna* promise?

Bob   Well, you'll no' get your job back.

Jock   So that's the way o' it, they've got their foot on oor necks, and they're gaun to put on the screw. Chuck up the Union! The men'll never agree to that.

Bob   What else can they dae?

Jock   They can go on the dole. We micht be better on the dole onyway.

Bob   By gee! That's a good idea, I never thoucht o' that. Dinna go near the pit, Faither, we ha'e nae buits or claes to start oor work wi' onyway. (*At mirror.*) My face is no' half broon, Faither.

Jock   They'll soon take the broon off your face: they'll soon make a mushroom o' ye. It's a hell o' a job, hunger and rags, water and bad air, and up at fower o' clock on the cauld, snawy mornin's, and under the heel o' a set o' tyrants for starvation wages. And what can we dae, just suffer it oot and say naething.

Bob   I ken what's needed . . .

Lizzie   It's a revolution that's needed, Bob.

Jock (*to* **Bob**)   Did you see any signs o' Tam Pettigrew when you were doon the street?

Bob   Ay, he was comin' oot the pub. As drunk as a sodger.

Jock   I'm gaun to gi'e that yin a thick ear, that's what's gaun to happen.

Bob (*at window*)   Here he's comin', faither! He's comin' here! Will I lock the door?

Jock   No, let him come in, I'll mebbe sober him up a bit.

Bob   That booze is just a curse, the pubs should be a' shut.

Tam Pettigrew *passes the window singing.*

Tam (*off*)   Are ye in!

Jock   Come in!

Tam *enters, and stands at door.*

Tam   I'm up to gi'e ye a dram, Jock. I'm Tam Pettigrew, I gi'e a dram to wha I like and I take a dram . . . when I like . . . That's me!

Jock   Are you no' ashamed o' yoursel', Tam?

Tam   Ashamed o' mysel'! What the hell ha'e I to be ashamed o'? I take a dram when I like . . . and gi'e a dram to wha I like . . . that's me . . . and always has been me . . . see!

Jock *goes to help him to chair.* **Tam** *pushes him from him.*

Tam   You surely think I'm drunk. I can manage to the chair myself. (*Walks unsteadily to chair.*) I'm Tam Pettigrew . . . I take a dram when I like . . . and gi'e a dram to wha I like . . . that's me!

He sits down.

Gimme a glass, Jock, and I'll gi'e ye a dram.

Jock (*to* **Bob**)   Rin doon and tell Kate he's here; she'll likely be anxious aboot him.

Tam   What's that? Anxious aboot me? I know what am dain', there's naebody need to be . . . anxious aboot me . . . Bob! Here's something for fags.

Bob (*at door*)   You shairly think I'd take money frae you. If I was Kate . . .

Jock   Rin awa' doon.

Bob *goes out,* **Lizzie** *following, looking at* **Tam***, half afraid.*

Tam   Anxious aboot me! Aboot *me*! Here, Jock, are you tryin' to be funny? . . . If you are, it's no' gaun to work, see? I'm Tam Pettigrew, and there's nae man tryin' to tak' his nap aff me, see!

Jock   D'ye think you're playin' the game, Tam?

Tam   D'ye want a dram, or dae ye no'?

Jock *loses his temper and snatches the bottle from* **Tam**'s *hand.*

Tam (*rising*)   Here! . . . what's the game?

Jock *forces him to his seat.*

Jock   Sit doon, see? I ha'e something to say to you.

Tam *struggles, and* **Jock** *has to raise the bottle to strike him.*

Jock   SIT DOON!

Tam *sits, afraid, and much sobered.*

Jock   A fine sicht you to cheer the he'rts o' your bairns, a lot o' he'rt'nin' a drunk faither'll gi'e them. See here, Tam. This conduct'll no' dae: you've got to pull yoursel' thigither; be a man, it's only cowards that droon their sorrows in the pub. Ha'e some respect for the wife you laid to rest.

There is a pause.

Tam   Jock, my he'rt's broken.

He buries his head in his hands.

Jock   Yours is no' the only he'rt that's broken, there's a hoosefu' doon by. And Kate's needin' a' the help you can gi'e her, or there's gaun to be anither death in the hoose.

Tam   I'll never get the better o' this, Jock . . . Died o' starvation . . . Them and their strike . . . they've killed her.

Jock   Noo, noo, Tam, it'll no' dae to lose he'rt that way, it canna be helped noo, and you'll need to put a stout he'rt to a stey brae.

Tam   It *could* ha'e been helped! Them and their bloody strike! The best woman that ever lived. Hoo can I get ower it?

Jock   You'll never get ower it if you're gaun to booze. You ha'e you're bairns to care for noo. *You've* got to take the mither's place, and you'll need to get ower it for their sakes. D'ye think the wife would rest in her grave if she kent o' this cairry on the day?

Tam   Them and their strike . . . Oh! Jock . . .

Enter **Kate**, *followed by* **Jenny** *and* **Bob**.

Kate   Come awa' doon, Faither.

Tam (*after a pause*)   Are you angry wi' me, Kate?

Kate   No' me. Come awa' doon and we'll ha'e a cup o' tea.

Tam   Kate, lass, I'm no' playin' the game. Tell me you're no' angry wi' me.

Kate   No, I'm no' angry wi' ye. Come awa' doon, the weans are wearyin' on ye.

Tam   Kate, I'm no' playin' the game

Jock *helps* **Kate** *to get* **Tam** *on his feet.*

Tam   Jock, she likes her mither.

Jock   Ay, ay, Tam. Awa' doon wi' her and get a cup o' tea and you'll soon be as richt as the mail.

Tam   *You're* no' angry wi' me, Jock?

Jock   No' me, Tam.

Tam (*going out with* **Kate**)   Them and their strike . . . them and their bloody strike! . . .

Jenny *follows.*

Jock   God guide ye, Kate, for you ha'e a big battle in front o' ye.

Bob   The booze is just a flamin' curse.

Jock   It's a pity for him tae, Bob.

Bob   It's *nae* pity for him, he's a washoot. May I choke mysel' stane deid the first time I put that stuff in my mooth.

Jock   It's easy speakin', but we're no' a' made o' steel. You're young yet, Bob and you ha'e a lot to come through before you can say what you can dae.

He sits at fire.

Bob   Kate's far too saft wi' him, it's a slap on the kisser he needs.

Jock   Awa' and meet your mither, she'll be on her road hame noo.

Bob   I ken what I should be done wi' it a'.

He lifts bottle from table, and, unseen by **Jock***, goes out and smashes it against a wall.* **Jock** *jumps on hearing the crash.* **Bob** *enters, rather proud.*

Jock   What the flames was that?

Bob   That's the stuff to gi'e them, poor it doon the street.

Jock (*looking at table*)   Here! Is that you broken that bottle o' whisky?

Bob   Too true, it's a pity there's only yin.

Jock   Well, I'll be damned. (*Loudly.*) Are you aware a bottle o' whisky costs thirteen shillin's, and here you've sent it sailin' doon the street. Ye flamin' imp!

Bob (*retreating*)   But I thoucht you said –

Jock   What did I say?! WHAT DID I SAY?! Thirteen shillin's worth rinnin' doon the street.

Bob   Was you wantin' to pour it doon your ain neck?

Jock   Shut up, ye flamin' agitator, before I lose my temper wi' ye. Thirteen white shillin's worth rinnin'. Oot o' my sicht, see, before I mulligrize ye!

Bob   By gee! It's great, richt enough: tellin' a man aff because he was drunk, and shootin' oot your neck noo because you canna get the same chance.

Jock *makes a mad rush after* **Bob***, who scoots.*

Jock   Never heard tell o' such a dirty trick a' my flamin' days. Thirteen white shillin's worth . . . ach! It's enough to break a body's he'rt.

Jenny *enters.*

Jenny   Faither, you'll need to go doon beside that man, he's still ravin' aboot the strike.

Jock (*putting on coat*)   A damned guid thumpin' is what *he's* needin'. (*Going out.*) Thirteen white shillin's worth rinnin' doon the street.

Jenny *sits at fireside, and, after looking into the fire for a while, takes a letter from her bosom. The canary sings merrily in the quietness.* **Lizzie** *enters and* **Jenny** *hides the letter again in her bosom.*

Lizzie   Jenny, Wull Baxter wants to see ye.

Jenny   Where is he?

Lizzie   He's standin' roon' the corner o' the hoose.

Jenny   Tell him to come in.

Lizzie *goes out.* **Jenny** *walks nervously round room. She is facing the fire when* **Wull** *enters. He halts at door.*

Wull (*softly*)   Jenny.

Jenny *turns and straightens herself.*

Jenny   What d'ye want here, Wull?

Wull   I'm gaun awa' the morn, Jenny.

Jenny   Weel!

Wull   I canna go without sayin' guid-bye!

Jenny   There was nae need, Wull.

Wull   You're gey hard, Jenny.

Jenny   No, Wull, I'm no' hard, you played a gey hard game wi' *me.*

Wull   I thoucht I was daein' richt, Jenny. I thoucht the men would make a start if somebody took the lead.

Jenny   And you stabbed them in the back; the neebours you ha'e lived wi' a' your days, the men you ha'e kept company wi', the men you ha'e sported wi . . . ye traitor!

Wull *is stung by the thrust, and* **Jenny** *relents.*

Jenny   Oh, Wull, what made you dae it? We were happy . . . ower happy . . . and noo . . .

Wull   We can be happy yet, Jenny. Let us gang awa' thigither . . . awa' frae here . . . awa' where nobody kens me . . . where we'll get peace.

Jenny   It's ower late, Wull, I canna forgi'e ye.

Wull   It was to let us get to Canada, Jenny. It was for your sake.

Jenny *looks into the fire, but makes no answer.*

Wull   I made a mistake, Jenny, I see that noo, but it's no' ower late to forgi'e me, and let us start a new life . . . The auld days were happy days, Jenny, I could go about wi my heid in the air, and everybody had a smile for me. But noo . . . everybody has a scowl and a curse . . . God, but I ha'e come through hell.

There is a pause.

It was the strike to blame, Jenny.

Jenny (*still looking into fire*)   Ay, the strike . . . the strike . . . shattered hopes and broken he'rts.

Wull   We can be happy yet, Jenny.

Jenny   It's ower late, Wull.

Wull   The strike'll soon be forgotten.

Jenny   Ay, but you failed me, failed us a', *that* can never be forgotten.

Wull   If I was to send for you after a while, Jenny . . .

Jenny   It's ower late, Wull . . . (*Holding out her hand.*) Guid-bye!

Wull   Think it ower for a while . . .

Jenny   Guid-bye!

He shakes hands with her, and then goes slowly away. **Jenny** *looks into fire.* **Wull** *halts at door, watches her for a second or two, then goes out. The bird sings blithely. After a pause,* **Bob** *enters.*

Bob   Here! Was that Wull Baxter in here?

Jenny *makes no answer.*

Bob   What was he dain' in here, I'm askin'?

Then he sees that she is upset.

What's wrang wi' ye, Jenny? Are ye vexed because he's gaun awa'? I wouldna be vexed; he's just a dirty, rotten, blackleg.

Jenny   For God's sake, Bob . . .

Bob   I wouldna vex mysel' like that.

Jenny   Ay, you would vex yoursel' tae, Bob; hunger and rags we can get ower but no' the likes o' this . . . Every dream and every hope shattered into a thousand bits. Oh! Is there to be nae peace . . . Ha'e we ay to be crushed, and crushed, and never get a chance to live! Ha'e we ay to be gropin' in the darkness? Nae sunshine ava! Oh God, dae something to tak' the load off oor shouthers or we'll gang mad!

She goes to room. **Bob** *watches her go in wonderment. Then* **Jean** *and* **Jock** *and* **Lizzie** *enter,* **Jean** *carrying a laden basket.*

Jean   If we had eggs, we could ha'e ham and eggs the noo, if we had ham, eh, Bob?

Bob   Did you mind my Woodbines?

Jock *cuffs his ear off the chair.* **Jean** *hands* **Bob** *his Woodbines.*

Lizzie   Is the strike finished, Daddy?

Jock (*taking her on his knee*)   Finished, dearies, and we ha'e got knocked oot again.

Jean (*putting groceries out on table*)   Ay, but we're no' gaun to lose he'rt, Jock; we'll live to fight anither day; there's life in the auld dog yet.

Then the sound of voices can be heard singing in the distance; the tune is 'The Red Flag'. A look of pride comes into **Jean**'*s eyes, and she listens. Then she speaks, as if inspired by some great hope.*

Jean   That's the spirit, my he'rties! Sing! Sing! Tho' they ha'e ye chained to the wheels and the darkness. Sing! Tho' they ha'e ye crushed in the mire. Keep up your he'rts, my laddies, you'll win through yet, for there's nae power on earth can crush the men that can sing on a day like this.

In Time O'Strife

The 2013 adaptation by Graham McLaren

The adaptation

I am delighted that such an important play from such a significant Scottish artist is back in print, and I am proud to have played a part in making that happen. What haunts me is the idea that all adaptations are by their very nature a reduction of the original, which in some ways I think I believe. Why then did I choose to adapt Joe Corrie's *In Time O' Strife*?

To answer that I must take you to 2011. Among my first projects as Associate Director for National Theatre of Scotland I directed another significant Scottish play, Ena Lamont Stewart's *Men Should Weep*. I also ran a series of events for the company entitled 'Staging the Nation', where we attempted to chart some of Scottish theatre's fragmented history. One of the very first events in the series was suggested by the playwright Peter Arnott, who said he would like to celebrate the play that influenced him most as a young artist, Joe Corrie's *In Time O' Strife*. If I'm being honest I, like many of my peers, knew the title but not the play itself. I knew that it was produced by John McGrath's 7:84 in the early 1980s, perhaps in the same year Thatcher's government decimated the miners. I knew that it had been published and uncovered by Linda McKenny, the same brilliant mind that unearthed *Men Should Weep* for 7:84. Therefore when it was suggested we investigate it, I got very interested.

In September 2011 we invited Peter Arnott to lead a rehearsed reading of *In Time O' Strife* and that day I found myself bothered by a question; why do these plays not get produced? Not ever. Other than the 7:84 production, I can't find record of any other Corrie play being professionally produced. This seemed incredible to me sitting among the spellbound audience watching this reading. Surely what we have in plays from Corrie, Stewart and others are excellent home grown 'angry kitchen sink dramas' which pre-date John Osborne's supposed invention of the genre by decades. Why then didn't we celebrate this? Was it because it was made in Scotland? Was it because these plays dealt with the struggle of the working class?

Afterwards I found myself comparing the play to Lorca or Synge. 'Are you suggesting we produce it?' asked Vicky Featherstone, then Artistic Director of the National Theatre of Scotland . I wasn't sure that I wanted to repeat the formula of *Men Should Weep*, 'And besides,' I said, 'I think the play promises a little more than it delivers, it feels like an early draft of a truly great play.' The idea then came that if it really was a play like those of Synge and Lorca it could perhaps stand up to a reimagining. I eventually plucked up the courage to ask Morag Corrie if she would permit me to adapt her father's play. I planned to use fragments of his other plays (there are over fifty to choose from) and some of his poems to implement the alterations that dramaturg Iain Heggie and I had identified. The plan was to use his poems as songs and choruses, adapt the scenes to focus on the personal struggle of fewer characters, to create a piece that perhaps owes as much to the Scottish theatre tradition of work that is popular in form and political in content as ever it owes to its kitchen sink roots.

At the time of writing this I have no idea what the final results of this endeavour will be, but without Morag Corrie's support and access to her father's work, including unpublished workbooks, I would not have embarked upon this project. I would not have become so obsessed with Corrie. Corrie the poet, the playwright and the miner who, while on strike in 1926, wrote a play not for fame or critical acclaim but to raise money for the soup kitchens feeding the miners and their starving families. His Bowhill miners' production became an international success, but his work was subsequently rejected by the Scottish Theatre establishment for being too working class. His poetry was described by T.S. Elliot as the greatest since Burns, but his career seldom progressed beyond the amateur circuit. I started to hope that perhaps this project could in some small way reignite an interest in Corrie as both an artist and as a significant figure in Scottish theatre history.

I am reliably informed by those who knew him best that Joe would have hated anyone altering even a syllable of his work, and of course we will never know what he would have made of this adaptation, but I honestly could not allow this man and his work to remain forgotten to all but a few historians. This adaptation is my genuine attempt not only to serve *In Time O' Strife* but also to capture the spirit of his many other works.

I am proud to be part of a National Theatre in Scotland which not only draws attention to our near-forgotten artists but now provides a home for theatre artists to ensure that in the future such talent is not so easily forgotten.

Graham McLaren
Associate Director, National Theatre of Scotland
October 2013

Interactive Footnotes

Graham McLaren's adapted script of *In Time O' Strife* contains interactive footnotes. These footnotes enable you to view video content about the making of the production on your smart phone or tablet. Follow the instructions below to download the National Theatre of Scotland Scanner app and scan the photographs to get further insight into how the production has been adapted.

How to use this Interactive Playtext

> National Theatre of Scotland Scanner is a free app that enables you to take a look behind the scenes and watch video clips about the making of the show.

> Visit the Apple App Store or Google Apps Marketplace on your smart phone or tablet.

> Search for 'National Theatre of Scotland Scanner' and download the app.

> Open the app and hold your phone or tablet above any of the photographs throughout the script.

> The app will scan the photograph and show you a video relating to that section of the play.

The National Theatre of Scotland in association with ON at Fife first presented *In Time O' Strife* on 3 October 2013 at Pathhead Hall, Kirkcaldy.

CAST

Jenny	Hannah Donaldson
Tam	Tom McGovern
Kate	Vicki Manderson
Jock	Ewan Stewart
Bob	Paul Tinto
Jean	Anita Vettesse
Wull Baxter	Owen Whitelaw
Lizzie	Luci Lang/Leila Donaldson

CREATIVE TEAM

Adaptation, Director and Designer Graham McLaren
Choreographer Imogen Knight
Composer and Musical Director Michael John McCarthy
Lighting Designer Lizzie Powell
Dramaturg Iain Heggie
Associate Designer Rebecca Hamilton
Trainee Assistant Director Andrew McGregor
Casting Director Anne Henderson
Casting Associate Laura Donnelly

BAND

Michael John McCarthy, Jennifer Reeve, Adam John Scott, Jonny Scott

The Scottish Government
Riaghaltas na h-Alba

The National Theatre of Scotland is core funded by the Scottish Government. The National Theatre of Scotland, a company limited by guarantee and registered in Scotland (SC234270), is a registered Scottish charity (SC033377).

Producer Pamela Walker
Production Manager Kevin Murray
Company Stage Manager Sarah Scarlett
Deputy Stage Manager Rachel Godding
Lighting Supervisor James Gardner
Sound Supervisor/Musical Arrangement Assistant Stevie Jones
Wardrobe Supervisor Janice Burgos
Wardrobe Technician Jerry Cook
Technician Neil Dewar
Digital Affiliate Eve Nicol
Chaperone Rebecca Petford

About the National Theatre of Scotland

It is our ambition to make incredible theatre experiences for you, which will stay in your heart and mind long after you have gone home.

We tirelessly seek the stories which need to be told and retold, the voices which need to be heard and the sparks that need to be ignited. We do this with an ever-evolving community of play makers, maverick thinkers and theatre crusaders. We try to be technically adventurous and fearlessly collaborative. We are what our artists, performers and participants make us. And with no stage of our own we have the freedom to go where our audiences and stories take us. There is no limit to what we believe theatre can be, no limit to the stories we are able to tell, no limit to the possibilities of our imaginations.

All of Scotland is our stage, and from here we perform to the world. We are a theatre of the imagination: a Theatre Without Walls.

Characters

Jock Smith, *a miner, forties*
Jean Smith, *his wife, forties*
Jenny Smith, *their daughter, twenties*
Bob Smith, *their son, twenties*
Tam Pettigrew, *a miner living next door to Jock, forties*
Kate Pettigrew, *his daughter, in love with Bob, twenties*
Wull Baxter, *a miner engaged to Jenny, twenties*

Left to right: Adam John Scott, Jennifer Reeve, Jonny Scott, Michael John McCarthy.

The audience enter on to the set: an old community hall with a low stage at one end. On the stage is a band who play as the audience enter and stand around the space. When the audience are assembled the band stop playing and the singer speaks.

Singer   One hundred and twenty years ago Joe Corrie was born. Fourteen years after that he started working as a miner. In 1926, after the General Strike, the miners were locked out of their pits unless they accepted lower wages and longer hours. They refused and went without wages for seven months. In that time Joe writes plays to raise money for the local soup kitchens to feed the miners and their starving families. After the strike he writes *In Time O' Strife* and he starts it with this song:

> We'll hang every blackleg to the sour apple tree,
> We'll hang every blackleg to the sour apple tree,
> We'll hang every blackleg to the sour –

SONG I: THE LOVER

Here in the guts of the earth – in my father's tomb;
In the forests of the past – in the gas and the gloom;
Naked, and blind with sweat, I strive and I strain;
Helpless, and racked to the heart with the hate and the pain.

But home, I will wash me clean, and over the hill,
To the glen of the primrose and the daffodil;
I will sing of my love so tenderly,
Even the lovelorn gods will envy me.

This is one of the nights I want to take the road
Away from sorrow, disease and the master's hold,
My heart cries out to be free but I must tend the machine,
Only a dream in my mind – blue, yellow and green
. . . The love-lorn gods will envy me.

During the dance the company encourage the audience to their seats at the other end of the hall.

Back row, left to right: Adam John Scott, Jennifer Reeve, Jonny Scott,
Michael John McCarthy. Front row, left to right: Vicki Manderson, Owen Whitelaw,
Hannah Donaldson, Paul Tinto, Tom McGovern, Ewan Stewart, Anita Vettesse.

DAY 185 ON STRIKE

Scene One

Jenny   You're lookin' awfu' pleased wi yersel, Wull Baxter.

Wull   No' me!

Jenny   Ay you! What's thon you're cairtin' aboot wi' ye?

Wull   Ach, it's only a wee mindin' for ye!

Jenny   But you've been oot on strike for six months, Wull. You an' a' the ither miners! You've nae money.

Wull   You're worth more than any amount of money, Jenny. Here.

He gives her the wrapped present.

Jenny   You're ower good tae me.

Wull   Open it.

She opens it, at length, as she speaks.

Jenny   You're that saft, you! Presents in the middle ay a strike! More money than . . . (*The fiddle appears.*) It's my fiddle. I can hardly credit it. Ma beautiful' aul' fiddle. Oh Wull. How did you get haud ay this?

Wull   Ach, mind yer ain business how ah goat it.

Jenny   But my faither put this awa' in the pawn weeks ago.

Wull   More's the pity! Lift it up, Jenny. Oan ye go!

Jenny   You shouldny have done this, Wull. (*She fingers it lovingly.*)

Wull   I couldny abide thinkin' o' it lyin' rottin' in the pawn one more minute. Each time I thocht o' it I thocht o' you breakin' yir heart the sad day your faither pawned it off. Lift it up. Oan ye go!

Jenny (*she does*)   Och, Wull.

Wull   The strike'll be ower soon. Fer it canny last much langer surely tae God. An' I had a wee bit put by.

Jenny   Yer ower guid tae me, Wull Baxter. But you'll ha'e tae take it back.

Wull   Ah'll no' be takin' it back, Jenny. You'll nae get tae play us a jig at oor weddin' if you've nae fiddle!

Jenny   I love you, Wull. But yer a big saftie.

Wull   When we get married the whole village'll be dancing.

Jenny   Ah'm doubtin' if ye even ha'e the sense ye were born wi'. Ye ha'e nae money and ye bide wi' your mither yit.

Wull   They'll be talkin' aboot oor wedding for years tae come.

Jenny   We canna even think aboot gettin' mairried till the strike's ower and we're a' back on oor feet!

Wull   It'll be the best wedding this grey wee place has ever seen.

Jenny   How will we afford the best wedding the village has seen?!

Wull   I'm no' for spendin the rest o' my life doon the pit, Jenny. We'll get oot a' here awa' frae thae noises. If ye'll ha'e faith in me.

Jenny   I ha'e plenty o' faith in ye Wull Baxter. But that'll no' put food on the table.

Wull   I'll put food on the table, Jenny. Don't you worry aboot that. Noo play us a tune on yer aul' fiddle.

She does.

Jenny   Get oot o' here, ya big lump, afore my mither gets back and finds you've been wasting yer money on me.

Wull   I'll go if ye promise tae ha'e faith in me.

Jenny   Ay, I promise.

Wull *leaves and* **Jenny** *plays the fiddle. Enter* **Bob**.

Scene Two

Bob   Was that my mither?

Jenny   Wull Baxter. An' look what he brought me.

Bob   Ay, an' where does your sweetheart get the money tae redeem that aul' thing back frae the pawn?

Jenny   Never you mind.

Bob   What aboot some chuck then?

Jenny   What aboot it?

Bob   Weel, what aboot it?

Jenny   Is it no' time you were awa' to the Pairish soup kitchen?

Bob   I'm waitin' till the last the day, it's aboot time I was getting' some o' the thick stuff.

Jenny   Ay, wait till the last, and when you get doon there'll be nane left.

Bob   That'll be *my* funeral.

Jenny   Ay, but you'll be guzzlin' the dinner in here.

Bob   Some hope when *you're* there.

Jenny   When the strike's finished we'll ha'e ham and eggs every mornin'.

Bob   If we had eggs, we could ha'e ham and eggs the noo, if we had ham.

Jenny   Eh?

Bob   I'm sayin', if we had eggs, we could ha'e ham and eggs.

Jenny   What the flames are you talkin' aboot?

Bob *rattles on the bowl and whistles.*

Jenny   Oh, for God's sake stop that, it gets on my nerves.

Bob   I think I'll join the pipe band.

Has another rattle.

Jenny   You'll break that flamin' bowl. Are you gaun to stop it?

Bob *stops.*

Jenny   You'll need to wait till my mither comes hame, and mebbe efter she comes hame tae.

Bob   Did ye hear there's likely to be a break-awa' the morn?

Jenny   Wha telt you that?

Bob   Never you mind, but it's true.

Scene Three

Enter **Kate**.

Kate   I'm up to see if you're gaun to the soup kitchen dance the nicht, Jenny?

Jenny   Are you gaun?

Kate   I am.

Jenny   Where did you get the money?

Kate   Threepence for some auld jam jars. You should come, Jenny; it'll be a richt guid dance.

Jenny   My shoon wouldna stand it, Kate. Anither month o' this strike and we'll be gaun aboot naked.

Kate   It canna last much langer noo.

Jenny   This is the worst week o' it yet!

Kate   We dinna ken hoo to turn wi' it, we're clean knocked oot. We'll need to hunger noo till we get the Pairish relief in the morn.

Jenny   Twa weeks' work'll put us on oor feet again.

Kate   We've been saying that for the last six months.

Jenny   Has your mither seen the doctor yet?

Kate   Ach, him! He'll order her tae her bed and gi'e her a line for medicine. What guid is that when there is no' a penny in the house?

Jenny   But she's no' weel.

Kate   Ay, she is is gettin' tired, when the cough does stop she canna sleep for thinkin on the bairns. Pair wee things, they seem to ken, they just sit and look like wee lambs and never say a word gaun tae bed to sleep the hunger off them. But I'm finished worryin', it's a mug's game.

Bob   Tak' off your coat then, and sit doon.

Kate   There's some thinkin' aboot startin' back tae his work, I hear.

Bob   Ay, and your faither's yin o' them. Sit yersel' doon.

Kate   Wha said that?

Bob   He said it himsel' at the street corner. Sit, I'm sayin'.

Kate   Ay! Let him try it. Sit yersel'.

Jenny   He'll no' blackleg, Kate.

Kate   Ah'll knock his bloody heid aff.

Bob   He was ay a gaffer's man.

Jenny   Haud yer wheesht.

Kate (*to* **Jenny**)   Where's your faither?

Jenny   Lyin' in there wi' a fat heid. An' d'ye ken what he did yesterday?

Kate   No.

Jenny   Backed a double and came hame drunk as a lord, singin' like a canary. And no' a crust in the hoose. He met in

wi' some auld pal here on holiday frae America, so he says,
and didna come oot the pub till the double was spent.

Kate   Was your mither wild?

Jenny   Ay she put the singin' oot o' his heid.

Kate   Is she no' in?

Jenny   She's awa' looking for grub. That auld McIntyre the
grocer this mornin' says tae her 'I'll gi'e ye plenty, if you send
your man back to his work'.

Kate   And what did she say to that?

Jenny   She spat in his face.

Kate   That's the stuff to gi'e them. I canna understand the
tradesmen aboot here, they're a' up against the miners, but
bad conditions for the miners means bad conditions for them,
tae. They'll mebbe learn that some day when they're puttin'
up their shutters.

Bob

       When Rebel Tam was in the pit
       He tholed the very pangs o' Hell
       In fechtin' for the Richts o' Man,
       And ga'e nae thoucht unto himsel'.

       'If I was just in Parliament,
       By God!' he vowed, 'They soon would hear
       The trumpet-ca' o' Revolution
       Blastin' in their ear!'

       Noo he is there, back-bencher Tam,
       And listens daily to the farce
       O' Tweedledum and Tweedledee,
       And never rises off his arse.

Kate   An' are you gaun tae the dance tonight, Bob?

Bob   If I had money, Kate, I would be there and dance the
shoon right off ye.

Kate   An' what makes ye think I'd let ye?

Bob   How aboot a wee practice the noo?

Kate   What, here?

Bob   Dancin' wi' you these grey days in the grey houses, grey skies would make the mornin' sun flood us wi' gold.

Kate   Don't be so saft. Is it no' time you were awa' to the soup kitchen?

Bob   I'll take ma chances.

Oor Jenny has her fiddle back.

Kate   Ah thocht thon was away at the pawn. Hoo did ye get it back?

Bob   That sweetheart ay hers has been hoardin' money. Has he no', Jenny?

Jenny   Wheesht you!

Bob   Would you like to hear a tune, Kate?

Kate   Why no'? We're needin' something to cheer us up.

Jenny   You'll waken him.

Bob   What dae I care for him, when I have Thisbe robed in virgin white.

Kate   Oh, for God's sake you. Play something cheery, Jenny, and let's get a dance.

SONG 2: OOR JENNY

Oor Jenny doesna care a doo
For onything or ony body;
To meet a ghost she'd just say 'Boo!'
Syne draw a stick across its hurdie.

And Willie Turpie kent fu' weel,
Hoo harum-scarum was oor Jenny;
Yet he soucht her for his wife –
The quaitest lad in Forgandenny.

Left to right: Jennifer Reeve, Hannah Donaldson, Vicki Manderson, Michael John McCarthy, Paul Tinto.

Oh harum oh scarum
The flamin' temper o' oor Jenny;
Oh harum oh scarum
The flamin' temper o' oor Jenny.

But Jenny said, 'I want nae man!'
My mither thoucht that she was silly,
Jenny waved an angry han'
And said 'To hell wi' you and Willie!'

So sister Jean wi' love to spare,
Beguiled the lad frae Forgandenny –
Noo there's no' sowl no' sowl can bear
The flamin' temper o' oor Jenny.

Scene Four

Jock *comes in.*

Jock   Oh! Stop that! What kind o' dance d'ye ca' that? God kens what the world's comin' tae. Nae wonder you're a' knocked-kneed and in-taed getting.

Kate   Wha's in-taed?

Jock   The half o' ye are gaun aboot like a lot o' hens. How did that damned fiddle make its way oot o' the pawn?

Bob   It was her sweetheart.

Jock   You're damned lucky that can think aboot music and dancin'.

Bob   I doot he couldnae stand her long face withoot it.

Jenny   Haud yer tongue, Bob.

Jock   That was my place tae get that back, Jenny.

Jenny   I know, Faither.

Jock   Ay, damned lucky that can think aboot dancin'. Did you get a paper the nicht?

Bob   You're sittin' on it.

Jock (*brings it out*)   Where's the racing page? It's a' back tae front. (*Finds it.*) Where's your mither?

Bob   Awa' beggin', and lowerin' hersel' again till we get some money frae the Pairish in the morning: and there was nae need for it if you had played the game yesterday.

Jock   If the double had went doon what difference would it have made?

Bob   But the double came up, and you gied the winnin's to the publican to help him buy anither motor.

Jock   Hoo would you like to be me, Kate?

Kate   Onything fresh in the paper aboot the strike?

Jock   To hell wi' the strike. It should never have happened. I'm payin' nae mair Union money after this. I've got enough o' it this time. For thirty years I ha'e paid it, but never anither penny will they get frae me.

Kate   Wha're ye talkin' aboot?

Jock   Oor leaders. It's easy seen that this has a' been planned in Russia.

Kate   What makes you think that, Jock?

Jock   Look at the papers, you'll see pages aboot it every nicht. It's the Socialists to blame. It's a revolution they want.

Kate   D'ye mean to tell me, Jock, that you've been locked oot for six months and yet ye disna ken ony better than that?

Jock   It's you that doesna ken ony better. I was makin' fifteen shillin's a shift before they broucht us oot on strike, Jenny, they'll tell you that.

Kate   You must have been well in the know. My faither wasna makin' as much as feed a canary.

Jock   Fifteen white shillin's a shift and the best o' conditions at that.

Kate   Are ye a Mason?

Jock   No, I'm no' a Mason.

Kate   It's a mystery to me.

Jock   No, this 'Strike! Strike! Strike!' It'll no' dae.

Bob   But it couldna be helped.

Jock   Hoo could it no' be helped?

Bob   The maisters want to gi'e us less wages and make us work langer 'oors, what else could we dae but strike?

Jock   We could have knuckled doon.

Kate   But you're a Scotsman, Jock.

Jock   And prood o' it.

Kate   Doesna say much for Scotland.

Jock   Ay, it says mair for Russia. I ken what I would dae if I was the Gover'ment. I'd get a boat and ship the hale damned lot to Russia.

Bob   Wha, the coalmaisters?

Jock   No, thae Socialists and Communists.

Bob   But they didna reduce your wages!

Jock   I ken that fine.

Bob   And if you ken that fine, what is the argument aboot?

Jock   What I'm sayin' is, that we'd been far better if we had knuckled doon. I kent we were gaun to be defeated.

Bob   Wha said we were defeated?

Jock   Bob, we haven't earned a wage for six month and we've been deserted by the Unions, I ken when we are defeated.

Bob   D'ye ken onything aboot backin' doubles and gi'en the winnin's to the publican?

Jock   Oh here! We've heard enough aboot that, give it a rest.

Scene Five

Wull Baxter *enters.*

Wull   Hullo, Jock, could I have a word? (*To* **Kate**.) And how's your mither's health?

Kate   Not too bad, considerin' we're a' slowly fadin' awa'.

Wull   It's a fine nicht, Bob.

Bob   Is it?

Wull   Hullo, Jenny.

You're lookin' rather wild like, Jock. What's wrang?

Jock   Oh, we have been ha'in' an argument.

Wull   Ay. What's the trouble?

Jock   The strike.

Wull   We're thinkin' gey seriously aboot it noo. We werena expectin' it to last as lang as this.

Jock   A piece o' damned nonsense and thrawness. I've been tellin' them that I've paid my last penny to the Union.

Wull   I'm finished wi' the Union tae.

Bob   What's that you say, Wull?

Wull   The Union has failed us, Bob. They ken damned fine the battle's lost long ago, and they should have cried the strike off when the rest o' the industries went back tae work.

Bob   We've naething to lose noo, and we may as well fight to a finish.

Wull   If we saw ony signs o' the finish it wouldna be sae bad. But it's likely to go on for months yet, if it's left to oor leaders.

Bob   Weel, let it go on. The coalmaisters'll mebbe no' be sae keen to lock us oot again.

Wull   We dinna ha'e a very guid case, either. We can see noo that the pits havena been payin'.

Kate   Has that no' ay been their cry? Was that no' their cry when the women worked doon the pits?

Jenny   There wasna women worked doon the pits.

Jock   My faither was born doon the pit.

Jenny   Born doon the pit?

Jock   Ay, an' it's no' everybody can bum aboot that.

Kate   Something to bum aboot: a woman workin' doon
the pit till the very minute o' confinement. And still the pits
didna pay.

Jock   Ay, my granny carried coal up the auld stair pit for
mony a lang day. What's mair, she helped to lift the stane off
my grandfaither when he was killed.

Jenny   Is that true, Faither?

Jock   Helped to lift the stane off him; helped to cairry him
hame a corpse. And you're grumblin', Kate, but you dinna
ken you're alive. Frae daylicht to dark they tae work then; the
only time they saw daylicht was on the Sunday.

Kate   And still the pits didna pay.

Jock   I ken that fine, you didna need to tell me that.

Kate   And if the miners hadna foucht against it your women
micht have been workin' in the pits yet.

Jock   I ken that fine!

Kate   They had to fight to make things easier for us.

Wull   We're fightin' a losin' fight, Kate, you canna deny that.

Kate   We are, if a' the men are like you. But they're no', and
we're gaun to win yet.

Wull   It's too late in the day to win noo. And the sooner it
comes to an end the better for everybody concerned.

Kate   Mebbe you're yin o' them that wants to bring it to an
end.

Wull   I have been thinkin' aboot it, but I havena made up
my mind yet.

Bob   If you've been thinkin' aboot it, you've made up your
mind.

Wull   Weel, to tell you the truth, I didna see the use o'
carryin' on much langer.

Bob   Then you're no' the man I thoucht you were.

Wull   No?

Bob   I never thoucht you would stoop sae low as split on us.

Wull   I'm no' splittin'. But when word comes that the Pairish Cooncil is no' payin' ony mair relief, it's time something was done to bring it to an end.

Bob   What?

Kate   No' payin' ony mair relief! Wha tellt you that?

Wull   The cooncil had a meetin'. Nae Pairish money the morn, and a hunner polis in at the pit to smash up the pickets.

Kate   And Britons, never, *never* shall be slaves.

Bob   I've been expectin' it.

Jock   That'll put us in a nice mess.

Wull   It'll bring the issue to a heid, Jock. It'll end the strike here.

Kate   Starve the women and bairns to force the men back to their work. And you agree wi' that policy?

Wull   There's nae ither way that I see.

Kate   Ye traitor.

She attacks him.

Wull   I'll be in later, Jock, I want to ha'e a talk wi' ye.

Kate   Ay, awa' oot o' the sicht o' decent folk, ye scab!

Wull *goes.*

Kate   What d'ye think o' that, Jenny?

Jenny   I canna understand him, Kate.

Kate   Dinna break your he'rt ower him.

Jenny   I didna think he was yin o' thae kind.

Kate   You should get shot o' him.

Jenny   We are to get mairrit when the strike is finished.

Kate   Noo, noo, Jenny, dinna greet.

Bob   The dirty swine!

Jenny   I canna take this. I'm awa' efter him. (*She goes.*)

Bob   He has been in the office wi' the manager. If he goes to his work in the mornin' there'll be nothing left o' him.

Jock   Nae Pairish relief, that means nae soup kitchen. Hoo dae they think we're gaun tae live? It's murder!

Bob   And the likes o' Wull Baxter, a workin' man, agreein' wi' it.

Jock   No' a crust in the hoose the nicht, and nae hopes o' getting' ony the morn. Ach, I'm fed up wi' the hale blasted thing.

Jock *goes.* **Bob** *comforts* **Kate** *as* **Tam** *enters.*

Scene Six

Tam   Kate, are you gaun to stay here a' nicht?

Kate   What d'ye want?

Tam   Your mither's in her bed, that cough is gettin' worse, and I want you to get my pit claes ready.

Kate   Your what?

Tam   My pit claes. I'm gaun oot to my work.

Kate   And are we to have nae say in this?

Tam   Wha?

Kate   My mither and me?

Tam   What the hell have you to do wi' it?

Kate   D'ye think I could walk through the streets o' Carhill again if you blackleg? D'ye think my mither could speak to the neebours again?

Tam   It'll soon be forgotten.

Kate   Blackleggin' can never be forgotten.

Tam   But we're in utter starvation, that's what has put your mither to her bed. An' nae Pairish money the morn.

Bob   If we march a thousand strong tae the Pairish offices they'll pay oot the money.

Tam   The polis are there to keep us frae marchin'.

Bob   It takes mair than polis to stop a hungry mob.

Tam   I'm gaun tae my work.

Kate   An' you'll come hame to an empty hoose. I'd tramp the country and beg my crust than stay in the same hoose as a blackleg.

Tam   But something has to be done.

Bob   Fight on to the finish, that can be done.

Enter **Jock**.

Tam   Nae Pairish money the morn, Jock.

Jock   What are ye gaun to dae aboot it, Tam?

Tam   God knows. Will ye go back to the pit?

Jock   The pit'll come to me before I go to the pit. I'll stay awa' frae it noo, just for spite. Stop the Pairish relief, what the hell'll be their game?

Bob   There'll be a riot here the morn if they try to stop it.

Jock   A lot o' guid that'll dae.

Tam   Ay, a lot o' guid that'll dae, Jock; half o' us clouted wi' a polisman's baton, and landed in the jile.

Bob   It's mair honourable to be clouted wi' a polisman's baton than clouted wi' a miner's fist.

Jock   Ach, God kens what we have been broucht on to the face o' the earth for.

Kate   There's a guid time comin' yet, Jock.

Jock   It's been comin' a' my time, but it's a damned sicht farther awa' noo than ever it's been.

Tam   Ay, a body would be better deid.

Kate   Did you ever hear such a crowd o' men? And they wonder why they're losin' the strike.

Tam   You havena the responsibility o' a hoose on your heid.

Jock   Ay, they're young, Tam, and doesna ken what it means to the likes o' us.

Bob   Stick oot your chest, man! Fight like hell, and never say die till a deid horse kicks ye.

Jock   It's no' easy for a hungry man to stick oot his chest.

Tam   It is not, Jock.

Kate   Well, stick your fingers to your nose at them. Guid nicht.

Bob   I'll come wi' ye, Kate.

Kate *and* **Bob** *go out.*

Jock   God kens what's to be done. We have come through many a hard time o't, but never the likes o' this.

Tam   The wife's no' keeping weel ava, Jock: that cough o' hers is gettin' worse.

Jock   She'll need to take care o' hersel', Tam.

Tam   Tak' care o' hersel'! And hasna had a meal the day! I'll need to do something, Jock, I canna let things go on like this.

Jock   But what can you dae?

Tam   I can go to my work.

Jock   I wish I could help ye, but I'm needin' help mysel'

SONG 3: KEEP IN WITH THE GAFFER

For mony a year I ha'e wroucht doon below.
But never in bits that are wet or are low,
For I make it my business wherever I go
Ay to keep in wi' the gaffer.

I was just a bit laddie when plain I could see
That some had it easy, as easy could be;
So I thoucht to mysel' that the best thing for me
Was to try and keep in wi' the gaffer.

Keep in with the gaffer.
Keep in with the gaffer.
Yes it's fine fine fine fine fine
To keep in with the gaffer.

Noo, my boss at the time was a Mason o' men,
So I scrimpit and saved and hot seeven pound' ten,
Then bravely I bearded the goat in its den,
A' to keep in wi' the gaffer.

The next boss I had was a musical man,
He stood like a sodger and waggled the wand,
So I learned the cornet and played in his band,
A' to keep in wi' the gaffer.

The next was a cratur' o' different stamp,
A colonel-in-chief in the Salvation camp,
So I got him to 'save' me and I carried the lamp
A' to keep in wi' the gaffer.

The last was a punter – a horse-racin' man,
So I put doon my Bible, and followed his plan;
But it came to an end wi' my shirt in the pawn,
A' to keep in wi' the gaffer.

Scene Seven

Enter **Jean** *and* **Jenny**.

Jean   There's no' a grocer or baker in the toon'll gi'e me a crust.

Jock   Get oot my pit claes.

Jean   No, you came oot wi' your neebours, and you'll go back wi' them.

Jock   Have we to dee o' hunger?

Jean   Something'll turn up yet.

Jock   Oh! Ha'e some sense. What can turn up?

Jean *breaks down.*

Jenny   Ha'e ye nae he'rt! Barkin' at my mither like that when you ha'e mair need to be comfortin' her. For six months she has scraped through, and you've never kent what it was to want a bite or a smoke till the nicht; lowered hersel' mony a time to keep things gaun, and noo, when she's beat, you can only bark at her.

Jock   I dinna mean it, Jean.

Jean   I ken that, Jock, I'm no' worth a haet gettin'.

Jenny   Mebbe my uncle, John, would help us?

Jean   You're no' gaun near him. He's a blackleg,

Jock   John would help us if he kent we were in this hole.

Jean   Not supposin' we should dee.

Jock   Can we no' sell that fiddle?

Jean   We took it tae pawn already, Jock.

Jock   Ay, but Wull Baxter bought it back.

Jean   He surely did not?

Jock   He brought it back for oor Jenny.

Jean   We can hardly take it straight back tae them, Jock.

Jock   Something'll need to go.

Jean   That fiddle's no' gaun oot o' this house.

Jock   A fiddle that the lassie can hardly play.

Jean   I cannae watch her break her he'rt if she were to lose it again.

Jock   I'm gaun to the pit, I'll starve for nae man.

Jean   For God's sake, man, ha'e some sense.

Jock   It's you that has nae sense. You'd starve rather than hurt her feelings. (*To* **Jenny**.) Jenny, would you be vexed if we selt your fiddle? We'll get you anither yin when the strike's finished. Your mither has been in every shop in the toon and canna get a crust.

Jennifer Reeve.

Jean   Jock!

Jock   We're up against it, Jenny, and some o' us have to make a sacrifice.

Jean   You should have sacrificed your beer yesterday. An' this wouldna have happened.

Jock   You dinna need to tell me that, but it's past and canna be helped. Hoo are we gaun to get a crust o' breid, that's the question. Folk that ha'e toiled and battled a' their days, workin' frae hand to mooth, even in the best o' times, slaves, and to think we've to go back to that pit on worse conditions! It would be a God's blessin' if the roof came doon and crushed the life oot o' us, we'd be awa' frae a' the bloody sufferin'.

Jean   That's a selfish wey oot o' it, and it's selfishness and greed that's the cause o' a' the sorrow and sufferin' the day.

Jenny   You can sell it, Faither. Oan the condition that ye don't tell Wull.

Scene Eight

Wull Baxter *enters.*

Wull   Don't tell me what?

Jenny *leaves, upset, comforted by* **Jean**.

Wull   Weel, that was some row the nicht, Jock. Kate's a right starter, isn't she?

Jock   Ay, she has a temper.

Wull   Ye ken, it's the women o' this place that's keepin' this strike gaun on, but they don't ken what it's like. The coal! The coal! Get oot the coal! What does it matter if a man loses his sicht or his life. The country wants cheap coal, so get it oot! We are just machines that get oot the bloody coal. And yet it's the women that's gettin a' het up ower the heid ay it.

Jock   Ay. They seem to ha'e got their birz up.

Wull   Ye' know that we're thinkin' aboot, tryin' to get oot to Canada, efter the weddin'? It has alway been a dream o' oors, Jock. There's naething here for the young folk.

Jock   Ay, that would be great for ye' both but it's no' cheap gettin' oot there.

Wull   The men that are startin' the morn are gettin' a guid chance.

Jock   How's that?

Wull   Five pounds when they make a start and a pound a day.

Jock   That's the stuff, eh!

Wull   No' often the miner gets a chance like that.

Jock   Ye can hardly credit it.

Wull   Take it frae me, Jock. So what about it?

Jock   What aboot what?

Wull   Makin' a start in the mornin' wi' the rest o' us?

Jock   Eh! D'ye mean to tell me your canvassin' for blacklegs?

Wull   It's no' blackleggin. You ken as weel as me that if it's left to the leaders it'll never be finished. The place is in ruination: if the pit doesna open soon it'll never open. A week's work would put you on your feet again.

Jock   Would put wha on their feet?

Wull   Dinna be a daftie ower this, Jock. Yer big chance only comes yince in yin lifetime.

Jock   Money o' ony kind is a big temptation, but before I would touch their blood money I'd eat grass fae the roadside.

Wull   Are you feart for the Socialists and the pickets?

Jock   I don't want ony insults, Wull.

Wull   I thought you had mair pluck than that, Jock.

Jock   Ye flamin' twister! If ye insult me like that I'll choke the life oot o' ye.

Jenny *and* **Jean** *enter.*

Wull   I thought the wey you were speakin' –

Jock   Oot o' my sicht, ye traitor! And if I ever see Jenny speakin' to ye again, I'll cut your tongue oot o' yer heid. Oot o' that door, I say!

Wull *goes out.*

Jock   Jenny, I came oot like a man and I'll go back like a man; an' it'll never be said Jock Smith's a blackleg.

Scene Nine

Enter **Bob**.

Bob   Was Wull Baxter just here soundin' you aboot gaun to the pit?

Jock   He was.

Bob   Are you gaun, Faither?

Jock   Am I hell!

Bob   Isn't he a richt traitor? Did you think he was yin o' thae kind?

Jock   No, or he'd been coortin' some ither place. Will there be mony'll try to go oot?

Bob   I canna believe Tam Pettigrew was thinkin' aboot it tae.

Jock   If the Pairish doesna pay ower the morn I doot there'll be a big breakawa'.

Bob   The Pairish'll pay ower, or we'll tear doon the buildin'. We're formin' pickets for the morn, Faither; will you gi'e us a hand?

Jock   I will, and if Wull Baxter tries to pass me he'll ha'e a face without a nose. Is there onything I can dae the nicht?

Bob   There's a meetin' to discuss the plans for the morn.

Jock   That's the stuff to gi'e them! Blaw their blasted pits in the air, and the blacklegs wi' them. A pound a shift! No, son, I may sell my muscle, but I'll never sell my soul.

Jock *and* **Bob** *leave.*

Jean   We canna sell that fiddle, Jenny. Tak' this wedding ring instead.

Jenny   I canna let you pairt wi' that, Mither.

Jean   I can pairt wi' it easier than yer fiddle. Dinna argue. Hurry and bring up some groceries, you're a' hungry. Hurry, Jenny.

Jenny *goes.* **Jean** *sits.*

Jean   We were a prood pair that day, Jock. Blue skies and sunshine and the birds singin' on every ither tree. But that was lang, lang syne. nae struggle then, and nae tears, just sang and laughter. Ay, changed days noo, Jock.

SONG 4: THE PITHEAD LASS

I watch you passing down the street these grey days;
Grey houses, grey skies, and the pit-smoke's grey haze.
Jauntily humming an April air; and the morning sun
Floods with its gold an ancient street in Babylon.

And Thisbe, robed in virgin white, gaily does she pass,
Innocent of the tragic eyes of Pyramus.
I watch you passing down the street, these grey days;
And thinking of your mother's fate, my heart prays.

Anita Vettesse.

DAY 192 ON STRIKE

Scene Ten

Jenny   What d' ye want here?

Wull   I need tae speak awa' frae the rest of them.

Jenny   Have ye been doon the pit, Wull? I wouldn't ha'e thoucht it o' you. But mibbe it's no' too late. Go tae the men and say that ye made a mistake and you're sorry.

Wull   But I'm no' sorry, Jenny. All my life I've been in this village living in the shadows of yon wheels at the pithead. The same pithead where I held on tae my mither's shawl just a bairn, my heart full o' dread and fear as we watched my faither's body brought up in a canvas bag. My strong, kind, lovin' faither identified by the soldier's medal on his coat. One day that'll be me doon there and you prayin' for a miracle and I cannae dae it. I cannae. Ay. I saw a chance tae make some decent money for once and I took it. For the weddin', Jenny.

Jenny   How can there be a weddin' now?

Wull   I asked ye tae have faith. Tae trust me, Jenny. You'll see in twa weeks. I'll make a wheen pounds and we can get off to Canada. Canada, Jenny.

Jenny   Will ye' stop dreamin' on Canada?

Wull   A new country, clean air, a clean start, Jenny.

Jenny   You ken I've always wanted tae go there one day . . . but now . . .

Wull   Well, now I'll ha'e the money. Let's stop speakin' aboot leaving here and just dae it.

Jenny   I want tae believe we can be happy again, Wull.

Wull   We can be happy, Jenny, awa' frae here where naebody ken us.

Jenny   What'll everybody think?

Enter **Jean**.

Jean   A douchter o' mine gaun to Canada on blood money.
A fine thing that would be. Jock said if ever he saw ye speakin'
to Jenny he would cut the tongue oot o' yer head.

Wull   Think aboot it, Jenny. It's not ower late.

Jean   Get oot, ye traitor!

Wull *goes.*

Jean   Wull Baxter oot workin'! Cutting oor very throats. If
he ever comes aboot you again, Jenny, yer faither'll –

Jenny   I didna ask him to come, Mither.

Jean   I ken, and I'm vexed for ye.

Jenny   I love him, Mither.

Jean   Forget aboot him.

Jenny   He blacklegged for us tae get tae Canada.

Jean   I said forget aboot him.

Jenny   Oh, Mither. (*She breaks down.*)

Jean   Ay, ay, but things'll come a' richt for you yet, lass.

Jenny   I was lookin' forward to happy days, but everything
has a' gane crash and in the yin day.

Jean   There's naebody escapin' the strike, Jenny, we're a'
getting' a blow o' some kind. But we're learnin' and some day
we'll mebbe get oor ain back.

Scene Eleven

Enter **Jock**.

Jock   You should have heard the speech oor Bob made at
the meetin'.

Jean   What did he say?

Jock   'Fellow workers,' he says, 'are ye gaun to stand and see your wives and bairns starve to death before your e'en? Are you content to dae this and ca' yoursel's men? Fellow workers! We have been far ower meek in the past, the time has come when we've got to let them see that we're prepared to die.' He'd the blood boilin' in my veins. It was a great speech, Jean. Enough to break a body's he'rt.

Jenny   Have you heard wha it is that's workin'?

Jock   Ay, your Wull. He was at his work before the pickets were oot o' their beds.

Jean   Some pickets!

Jock   Weel, God pity him when he tries to get hame, he'll be torn frae limb to limb.

Jean   Jenny, I wouldna worry mysel' ower Wull Baxter, he's no' worth it.

Jenny   I'm no' worried, Mither, just disappointed.

Jock   Was he speakin' aboot gaun to Canada after the strike?

Jenny   We were baith gaun there. That's the reason he's workin'. I just canna understan' why he didnae wait.

Enter **Kate**.

Jean   How's your mother, Kate? Did she get a sleep last nicht?

Kate   No. An' there's been nae Pairish money for a week. We can't buy the medicine.

Jean   I'm sendin' for the doctor mysel', we're standin' nae mair o' this nonsense.

Jock   I would get the miners to mairch to London and blaw the Parliament in the air.

Jean   And where'll we be by the time you get to London?

Kate   I dinna ken what to do, Jean.

Jenny   Wheesht! We'll see if we can dae anything for ye.

Kate   The bairns are a' greettin' for something to eat, and I ha'e naething. God, but my mother is weary and just wants to lie doon and dee.

Jean   There's something gey far wrang wi' your mother. Go doon wi' Jenny and get her to bed. I'll see that you get something to tide ye ower.

Kate   I don't believe she has tasted a bite for days.

Jenny   This is hellish! And we can dae naething tae help, naething ava. And they wonder why we mairch in oor thousan's wavin' the red flag. If they could only suffer oor lot for a week they wouldna wonder sae much.

Jean *takes money from her purse and give it to* **Kate**.

Jean   She'll need to get a sleep or she'll be deid in the mornin'. If Dr Morrison's no' in, go for the ither yin, Kate.

Kate *goes out with* **Jenny**.

Jean   That cough is something deeper than a cauld.

Scene Twelve

Tam *enters*.

Tam   Is oor Kate awa' for the doctor?

Jean   She is.

Jock   Was you in the mairch to the Pairish Council this mornin'?

Tam   You'll no' get me takin' pairt in yon Bolshie stunts.

Jock   No, but you'll take the Pairish money when it comes.

Tam   Ay, *when* it comes.

Foreground: Ewan Stewart.

Jock We'll never get it sittin' at the fireside or lyin' on the grass. Were you no' on the pickets this mornin' either?

Tam I think mair o' my bed.

Jock Strikes are no' won in bed.

Tam Was you on the pickets?

Jock I was. Up at the pit at five o'clock.

Jean He's been singin' 'The Red Flag' since he came hame.

Jock This country's gaun to be a wee Russia if this strike lasts much longer.

Tam And would you like to see it a wee Russia?

Jock The sooner the better.

Tam You'd plenty to say against the Bolshies and Russia before.

Jock   Ay, but my brains has gone doon tae my stomach.

Tam   Weel, I don't want to see this country made into a wee Russia, it would bring ruination.

Jock   Ruination! That's the worst o' havin' three-course breakfast, it makes a man a hunner per cent Britisher.

Tam   If there's nae Pairish money the morn I'm gaun to work.

Jock   A man that's feart to mairch to the Pairish Council doesna ha'e the pluck to face the pickets. You'd been at your work this mornin' if you hadna been feart.

Tam   I ken, and so would anither hunner men in the place. It's the damned Bolshies that's keepin' us frae startin'.

Jock   And here's luck to them, says I.

Tam   And it's them that dinna want to work that's on the pickets.

Jock   D'ye mean that I dinna want to work?

Tam   I never mentioned you.

Jock   I was on the picket, and I'm damned sure I'll work beside you ony day.

Tam   Did I say you couldna'?

Jock   No, and you better no'.

Jean   You look like a pair that'll dee wi' the shovel in your hand. (*Handing him some bread.*) Here! Take this doon, and look slippy.

Tam   Did I say he couldna work, Jean?

Jock   Of coorse you did.

Tam   I did naething o' the kind.

Jean   Did I tell you to look slippy?

Tam   Oh, ay, take his pairt.

He goes.

Jock   Isn't he an agitator? Ay talkin' aboot work, and has never worked a' his days; he has starved his wife off the face of the earth.

Jean   I've lost about ten stane mysel' since I got mairrit.

Jock   You're a delicate lookin' cratur.

Jean   If it wasna for my guid nature I'd be a walkin' skeleton.

Jock   There's yin thing I admire aboot ye, Jean, and that's your pluck.

Jean   I'm glad you appreciate it.

Jock   I do, and I thank my lucky stars mony a time that I got the wife I did. As soon as the strike is finished we'll get oot your weddin' ring wi' the first money.

Jean   Let it stay where it is, we ha'e mair need o' the money than a ring on the finger.

Jock   I wouldna care if the strike was finished, it's been a hell o' a time.

Jean   You're no' gaun to be much better if you've to go back to the pit on the maisters' terms. It's been a hard time, richt enough, and money a nicht I have lain doon wonderin' where oor breakfast was to come frae, but, Jock, it's nae mair he'rtrendin' than watchin' thae wheels turnin' every day, and never lookin' oot the windie but dreadin' to see some o' ye cairrit hame a corpse or maimed for life. There are plenty o' women never bother their heids, they have seen that much and come through that much, that they have got hardened to it. But I havena reached that stage yet, na, thae wheels are ay between me and the sun, throwin' their lang, black shadows on the doorstep. It's mebbe been a time o' want since the strike started, but it's been a time o' peace; I was ay sure o' you and Bob comin' hame at nichts; but there's nae such faith when the wheels are turnin'. But you men dinna think o' thae things, you'll likely laugh at us when we tell ye aboot it.

Jock   It's a fact, Jean, we put nae value on oor lives.

Jean   You talk aboot a weddin' ring! I would gi'e the very he'rt oot o' my breist if I thought it would keep ye awa' frae that hell.

Jock   I'll need to try and get you awa' frae the pits, Jean, but it'll no' be easy noo they ha'e us gey weel chained, and I doot there's naething else for us but the same auld grind. Nearly seven months' rent on oor heids noo, and we're a' needin' buits and claes.

Left to right: Paul Tinto, Tom McGovern, Ewan Stewart, Anita Vettesse.

Left to right: Hannah Donaldson, Ewan Stewart, Tom McGovern, Vicki Manderson, Paul Tinto, Owen Whitelaw, Anita Vettesse.

The company forms a chorus.

> Women are waiting tonight on the pit bank
> Pale at the heart with dread,
> Watching the dead-still wheels
> That loom in the mirky sky,
> The silent wheels of Fate,
> Which is the system under which they slave.
>
> They stand together in groups.
> As sheep shelter in storm,
> Silent, passive, dumb.
> For in the caverns under their feet,
> The coffin seams of coal
> 'Twixt the rock and the rock,

The gas has burst into flame,
And has scattered the hail of Death.

Cold the night is, and dark,
And the rain falls in a mist.
Their shawls and their rags are sodden,
And their thin, starved cheeks are blue,
But they will not go home to their fires,
Tho' the news has been broken to them
That a miracle is their only hope.

They will wait and watch till the dawn,
Till the wheels begin to revolve,
And the men whom they loved so well,
The strong, kind, loving men,
Are brought up in canvas sheets,
To be identified by a watch,
Or a button,
Or, perhaps, only a wish.

And three days from now,
They will all be buried together,
In one big hole in the earth.
And the King will send his sympathy,
And the Member of Parliament will be there,
Who voted that the military be used
When last these miners came on strike
To win a living wage.

His shining black hat will glisten
Over a sorrowful face, and his elegantly shod feet
Will go slowly behind the bier.
And the director of the company will be there,
Who has vowed many a time
That he would make the miner eat grass.

And the parson, who sits on the Parish Council,
Starving the children and saving the rates,
Will pray in a mournful voice,

And tear the very hearts of the bereaved.
He will emphasise in godly phrase
The danger of the mine,
And the bravery and valour of the miner.

And the press
That has spilled oceans of ink
Poisoning the public against the 'destroyers of industry',
Will tell the sad tale,
And the public will say,

'How sad'.

But a week today all will be forgotten,
And the Member of Parliament,
The coalowner,
The parson,
The press,
And the public,

Will keep storing up their venom and their hatred,
For the next big miners' strike.

Women are waiting tonight at the pit-bank,

But even God does not see
The hypocrisy and the shame of it all.

Scene Thirteen

Enter **Kate**.

Kate   Is Bob in?

Jean   No.

Kate   Will there be ony chance o' me gettin' some money if
I go to the Pairish Clerk? I'll need to get some nourishment for
my mither. It's been a week withoot the soup kitchen and she's
beginnin' to rave aboot the bairns. Oh Jean! I dinna ken what
to dae.

Jock   It's your faither that'll need to go to the Pairish, Kate. They'll no' listen to you.

Kate   He'll no' gang.

Jock   He'll gang if I go doon to him, and in a hurry.

Jock *leaves.*

Jean   Where's the doctor?

Kate   Coming doon after he gets his dinner.

Jean   He'll gi'e her a bottle that'll make her sleep. She'll be a new woman in the mornin'. She's been worryin' hersel' ower much. We should have had the doctor lang syne, Kate.

Kate   Everything seems to be gaun wrang tigither.

Jean   It'll no' dae to lose he'rt, Kate. Wheesht! Lass, things'll come a' richt for us yet. I'll awa' doon to the hoose and get your faither to go to the Pairish Clerk; and I'll attend to your mither, till the doctor comes, you stay here and rest. Your mither'll be a' richt the morn', Kate, dinna worry aboot that. Here eat this.

Jean *gives her what little bread remains and goes.*

SONG 5: GRACE BEFORE FOOD

To ye who tame the earth
To ye who brave the sea
Ye toilers of the world who give this food to me
My blessings and my thanks in all humility

Scene Fourteen

Bob *enters.*

Bob   I'm wantin' a lend o' that poker.

Kate   What for?

Bob   A man's nae guid wi' his bare fists against a polisman wi' a baton.

Kate   I dinna want ye to get the jile. Did you see your mither?

Bob   I dinna want to see her. Is your mither nae better?

Kate   I need tae to ken who tae get some money frae the Pairish Clerk; oor bairns are in utter starvation.

Bob   If ye' gets a line frae the doctor ye'll get something.

Kate   Thanks, Bob. What way dae you no' want tae see yir mither for?

Bob   I'm likely to be arrested the nicht, Kate.

Kate   Hoo d'ye ken?

Bob   The sergeant o' the police warned me that if I took pairt in the demonstration against Wull Baxter and the rest I'd be arrested.

Kate   And are ye?

Bob   If we let them get hame withoot a demonstration there'll be mair men oot the morn. We've got to nip it in the bud, Kate.

Kate   Is it worth it, Bob? If it means the jile for ye? And the breakawa'll take place some time or ither. You nor onybody else can stem it, and you ken that, for it has happened before.

Bob   And it'll happen till the workers control their ain destiny. But we've got to fight till the last ditch every time, whether it means the jile or no'.

Kate   It'll hurt your mither and faither.

Bob   I ken it will, but I'll no' likely get ony mair than three months, and it'll be worth the sufferin' to ken I did my bit.

Kate   And you'll get a' your thanks for it in the yin day. The miners are a queer crowd, they forget about the fight when they got their first week's pay in their hand.

Bob   I ken a' that, Kate, but it has a' to be suffered, there's never onything won withoot a struggle. But I didna want tae argue wi' ye, I want tae say something to ye, Kate. I'm no' likely to see ye for a while noo.

Kate   What d'ye want tae say?

Bob   Will you stick to me, Kate?

Kate   Stay here, Bob, dinnae take pairt in the demonstration.

Bob   I was feart ye micht put me aff going, I dinna want tae quarrel aboot it. Tell me, Kate. Will ye stick tae me?

Kate   Ay, Bob, ye ken fine well I will.

Bob   Kate, whenever I get oot we'll get mairrit.

Kate   Is that richt?

Bob   I wanted to you gi'e you this. It's a wee thing I've been puttin off giving ye'.

Kate   What is it?

Bob   It's a wee broach I made. It's no' much, but it'll maybe mind ye o' me.

Kate   I wish you would put this affair aff, Bob. No, I dinna wish it either, for if you did you wouldna be the man ye are. But, Bob, you'll no' dae very weel in the jile, you're no' the jilebird type.

Bob   If my health doesna break doon, Kate, I dinna care. But never mind, my pithead lass, you keep your he'rt up till I come back.

Kate   I'll be waitin' on ye comin' back, Bob, ha'e nae fear o' that.

Bob   Weel . . . Guid-bye, Kate!

Kate   Guid-bye, Bob! This strike's gaun to break a' oor he'rts.

Bob *goes.*

Paul Tinto.

Scene Fifteen

Enter **Jock**. *He says nothing, but something is wrong.*

Kate   What's the maiter, Jock?

Jock   Oh, Kate.

Kate   What, Jock?

Jock   It's your mither . . .

Kate   What aboot my mither?

Jock   She . . .

Kate   Come on, Jock. What is it?

Jock   She's died!

Kate   Oh, Mammy!

Jock   Your faither's awa' to the Pairish wi' the doctor's line. But it's ower late noo. But Jean is doon there, wi' a' the bairns cryin' on their mither to speak.

Kate   Oh, Mammy. She gi'ed them the bite oot o' her ain mooth.

Jock   Christ knows what it's a' comin' tae, Kate.

Kate   I'll need tae go away back doon, Jock.

What can God be thinkin' aboot when he lets the like o' this happen? If it's God's will that has ta'en awa' my puir mither, he's a gey queer God, and doesna' ha'e much o' a he'rt for working folk it seems.

Kate *goes.*

Jock
    Some ca' this fate that comes by God's decree
    Then God must be the Fife Coal Company.

SONG 6: THE COMMON MAN

I am the Common Man, I am the brute, and the slave,
I am the fool, the despised, from the cradle to the grave.
I am the hewer of coal; I am the tiller of soil;
I am serf of the seas, born to bear and to toil.

I am the common man; but master of mine take heed,
For you have put into my head, oh! many a wicked deed.
I am the builder of halls; I am the dweller of slums;
I am the filth and the scourge when the depression comes.

I am the fighter of wars; I am the killer of men;
Not for a day, or an age, but again, and again, and again.

Scene Sixteen

Jenny *enters.*

Jenny   That's Wull Baxter up the pit, and he's comin' hame
between twa regiments o' polis!

Jock   Are there mony women there?

Jenny   Hunners, did you no' hear them booin'?

Jock   Could they not stay in their hooses and leave it to the
men?

Jenny   Oh, Faither, there's a riot started doon the street!
If we dinna get him awa' frae the polis they'll lynch him

Jock   God Almighty! Lock the door, Jenny.

Jenny's *undecided.*

Jock   Lock the door. He's no' getting in here.

Jock *goes to lock the door.* **Jenny** *holds him back.*

Jock   Oot o' my road, lassie!

Jenny *struggles.* **Jock** *loses his temper, and thrusts her aside as the
door bursts open, and* **Wull Baxter** *almost falls in, locking the door*

behind him. The mob is at his heels, shouting madly. A stone crashes through the window.

Jock   Oot o' this hoose!

Wull   Help me, Jenny. They'll kill me.

Jock   Oot o' here, you traitor!

Wull   They'll kill me, Jock!

Jenny   Why di' ye' come back here, Wull?

Wull   I cannae spend the rest o' my life like this, Jenny. I ken you feel the same. It was for us, Jenny.

Jenny   I dae feel the same, Wull, but no' betraying the miners.

Wull   The miners are caught between the maisters and the unions livin' on charity frae the Church. We're the common man. Do we no' deserve better than this? Do we no'?

Jock   Bloodshed! Bloodshed ower the heid o' you!

Wull   Naebody has died, Jock, I've no' killed anybody.

Jock   Have ye' no'? Kate's mither died not an hour ago. Starved tae death a' for the sake o' the strike. So the likes o' you can make a livin' wage.

Jenny   Oh, Faither, I didnae know.

Wull   That's naething tae dae wi' me.

Jock   Is it no'? Oot o' here before I crush the life oot o' ye! Open the door, Jenny.

She doesn't move.

Wull   I did it for us, Jenny. Help me. Don't send me oot there, Jenny. I know you feel the same as me.

Jock   Well, Jenny what's it to be?

Jenny *hesitates a second, then she goes to door, unlocks it, opens it. He goes.*

Jenny   Oh! Faither! What is wrong wi' me? Why dae I love him no matter what he does? Why does it hurt so much, Faither?

The women form a chorus.

> We have borne good sons to broken men,
> Nurtured them on our hungry breast
> And given them to our masters when
> Their day of life was at its best.
>
> We have dried their clammy clothes by the fire,
> Solaced them, tended them, cheered them well,
> Watched the wheels raising them from the mire,
> Watched the wheels lowering them to Hell.
>
> We have prayed for them in a Godless way,
> (We never could fathom the ways of God)
> We have sung with them on their wedding day,
> Knowing the journey and the road.
>
> We have stood through the naked night to watch
> The silent wheels that raised the dead,
> We have gone before to raise the latch
> And lay the pillow beneath their head.
>
> We have done all this for our masters' sake,
> Did it in rags and did not mind,
> What more do they want? What more can they take?
> Unless our eyes and leave us blind.

DAY 199 ON STRIKE

Scene Seventeen

Jean   There's word comin' ower the telephone when Bob's trial's finished.

Jock   I canna staun much mair o' this waitin'. They're no' tryin' him in the High Court before a jury o' auld farmers and

grocers and butchers to let him aff wi' a fine. I wouldna be
surprised if he gets six months.

Jean   What would he get six months for?

Jock   Ye seen the summons, they're just aboot chairgin' him
wi' startin' a rebellion.

Jean   But it was Wull Baxter that was the cause o' it, no'
oor Bob.

Jock   Ay, but Wull Baxter was helpin' the maisters, he was
dain' richt as far as they were concerned.

Jean   But the maisters are no' tryin' him.

Jock   Are they no'?

Jean   They're sayin' doon the street that they'll no' be ower
hard on him seein' that the strike's aboot finished. But there's
no' much sympathy wi' lawyers and judges, it's hard facts wi'
them a' the time, staring you through and through wi' their
cauld, grey e'en seein' a' the bad points, but very few o' the
guid yins.

Jock   It's true, Jean. Mebbe eichteen months for him, and
the strike likely to be finished the day. Oot for seven lang
months, hungered and starved just aboot off the face o' the
earth, just to go back defeated.

Jean   Ach! It's ay the same; you throw doon your tools, come
oot the pit, and stand at the street corner till you starve
yoursel's back to the pit again.

Jock   The next strike'll no' be sae quiet.

Jean   The next strike! You'll be breakin' your necks rinnin'
up to the pit to get your jobs before the strike's finished.

Jock   It was the leaders that let us doon.

Jean   And wha puts the leaders there? Hoo often dae ye
attend the Union meetin's? You tak' nae interest in your

affairs till there's a strike on, then you find oot you want new leaders. You get the leaders you deserve.

Jock   There's a lot no' interested, right enough; of coorse it's a' for the want o' sense.

Jean   It's the want o' sense that makes ye buy that paper you're readin'.

Jock   Eh?

Jean   That's a coalmaisters' paper.

Jock   You dinna need to tell me that.

Jean   Then what dae you buy it for?

Jenny *enters.*

Scene Eighteen

Jenny   Ha'e you heard aboot oor Bob? Mither, I ha'ena very guid news for ye. You'll need to bear up. Three years, Mither, They have him awa for three years. Oh Faither, he's got three years.

Jock   Good God! That's cruel.

Jean   That canna be true.

Jenny   It's true, Mither,

Jock   And we live in a civilised country. If this is civilisation put me in among the savages. Even God does not see the hypocrisy and the shame of it all.

Jean (*to* **Jenny**)   Does Kate ken?

Jenny   No. Will you go doon and tell her, Faither?

Jean   Here she's comin'.

Kate *enters.*

Kate   Here, Jean. (*Hands over money.*)

Jean   What is it, Kate?

Kate   Just a wee bit help.

Jean   But you ha'e mair need o' it than me.

Kate   You have pawned everything you have. Jenny has lost her fiddle again. And my faither got insurance money. Tak' it.

Jean   I'll pay it back when the strike's finished.

Kate (*to* **Jock**)   Ha'e you seen my faither today?

Jock   No' me, Kate.

Kate   He went oot after breakfast time, and he's no' hame yet. He cam' hame gey fu' yesterday. (*To* **Jenny**.) Hoo d'ye think Bob will get on?

Jenny   They'll be ower hard on him, Kate.

Kate   Will he get off?

Jock   I doot he'll no' get off.

Kate   Is the word in?

Jock   I dinna ken, Kate, I havena heard onything.

Kate   You *ha'e* got word. Tell me, Jock. Tell me, Jean.

Jean   Kate, they ha'e him awa' for three years.

Kate   Three years! Three years! And the miners are feart for revolution. Ha! ha! ha! Three years!

Jenny   C'mon Kate, I'll tak' ye hame.

Kate *and* **Jenny** *go.*

Jean   She's gettin' *her* share o' the strike. You'll need to ha'e a word wi' her faither, Jock. A' this boozin'll no' dae at a time like this.

Jock   He's ay been a washoot: least excuse and off on the beer. Best wife in the country, tae, but dinna seem to ken it.

Jean   He'll ken noo she's awa'.

Jenny *returns.*

Jock   What's wrang?

Jenny   They're flockin' up to the pit in their hunners to get their jobs back. There's a notice up at the pit that every man has to go before the manager before he gets his job back. Every man has to promise to chuck up the Union.

Jock   Oh! And if we *dinna* promise?

Jenny   You'll no' get your job back.

Jock   They've got their foot on oor necks, and they're gaun to put on the screw. Chuck up the Union! The men'll never agree to that.

Jenny   What else can they dae?

Jock   They can go on the dole.

Jenny   Ay dinna go near the pit, Faither, you ha'e nae buits or claes to start your work wi' onyway.

Jock   It's a hell o' a job, hunger and rags, water and bad air, and up at fower o' clock on the cauld, snawy mornin's, and under the heel o' a set o' tyrants for starvation wages.

Scene Nineteen

Tam Pettigrew *enters, singing.*

Tam   Are ye in?

Jock   Come in!

Tam   I'm up to gi'e ye a dram, Jock. I'm Tam Pettigrew, I gi'e a dram to wha I like and I take a dram when I like.

Jock   Are you no' ashamed o' yoursel', Tam?

Tam   What the hell ha'e I to be ashamed o'? I take a dram when I like and gi'e a dram to wha I like. You think I'm drunk. I can manage to the chair mysel'. I'm Tam Pettigrew, I take a dram when I like and gi'e a dram to wha I like. Gimme a glass, Jock, and I'll gi'e ye a dram.

Jean (*to* **Jenny**)   Rin doon and tell Kate he's here.

Tam   There's nae need to tell Kate aboot me. I know what I'm daein'. (*To* **Jenny**.) Here's something for yoursel'.

Jenny   You think I'd take money frae you?

Jean   Rin awa' doon.

Jenny *goes.*

Tam   Ashamed o masel'. Ashamed o' masel'! Here, Jock, are you tryin' to be funny? Well, it's no' gaun to work. I'm Tam Pettigrew, and there's nae man tryin' to tak' his nap aff me. D'ye want a dram, or dae ye no'?

Jock *snatches the bottle from* **Tam***'s hand.*

Tam   Here! What's the game?

Jock   Sit doon. I ha'e something to say to you. SIT DOON!

A fine sicht you to cheer the he'rts o' your bairns, a lot o' he'rt'nin' a drunk faither'll gi'e them. See here, Tam. This conduct'll no' dae: you've got to pull yoursel' tigither; be a man, it's only cowards that droon their sorrows in the pub. Ha'e some respect for the wife you laid to rest.

Tam   Jock, my he'rt's broken.

Jock   Yours is no' the only he'rt that's broken, there's a hoosefu' o' broken he'rts doon by. And Kate's needin' a' the help you can gi'e her, or there's gaun to be anither death in the hoose.

Tam   I'll never get the better o' this, Jock. Died o' starvation. Them and their strike, they've killed her.

Jock   Noo, noo, Tam, it'll no' dae to lose he'rt that way, it canna be helped noo, Tam and you'll need to put a stout he'rt to a stey brae.

Tam It *could* ha'e been helped! Them and their bloody strike! The best woman that ever lived. Hoo can I get ower it?

Jock You'll ne'er get ower it gaun to booze. *You've* got to take the mither's place. You'll need to get ower it for the bairns' sakes.

Tam Them and their strike. Oh! Jock.

Enter **Kate** *followed by* **Jenny**.

Kate Come awa' doon, Faither.

Tam Are you angry wi' me, Kate?

Kate No' me. Come awa' doon.

Tam Kate, lass, I'm no' playin' the game. Tell me you're no' angry wi' me.

Kate No, I'm no' angry wi' ye. Come awa' doon, the bairns are wearyin' on ye'.

Tam Kate, I'm no' playin' the game.

Jock *helps* **Kate** *to get* **Tam** *on his feet.*

Tam Jock, she is like her mither.

Jock Ay, ay, Tam. Awa' doon wi' her and get a cup o' tea and you'll soon be as richt as the mail.

Tam *You're* no' angry wi' me, Jock?

Jock No' me, Tam.

Tam Them and their strike, them and their bloody strike!

Jock *takes* **Tam** *out* **Jean** *helps* **Kate** *leave.*

SONG 7: WILL NO ONE SING A SONG?

Will no one sing a song of such intensity
    to the men of all nations,
That will shatter this system
    of things to its very foundations?

That will open the eyes blind with Greed and Ignorance
    to the grandeur and glory
Of life, simple, wondrous, and grand as a fairy story?

Left to right: Anita Vettesse, Ewan Stewart, Tom McGovern, Vicki Manderson,
Hannah Donaldson, Paul Tinto, Owen Whitelaw.

DAY 203 ON STRIKE

Scene Twenty

Wull *enters.*

Jenny What d'ye want here?

Wull Did ye get my letter yesterday?

Jenny I burnt it.

Wull I made a mistake, I see that noo, but it's no' ower late
to forgi'e me.

Jenny   It is ower late, Wull

Wull   I'm begging ye, Jenny. Gi'e me another chance. I ken ye love me.

Jenny   Ay, I love ye, Wull, I just canna forgi'e ye.

Wull   I thoucht I was daein' richt, Jenny. I thoucht the men would make a start if somebody took the lead.

Jenny   And you stabbed them in the back; the neebours you ha'e lived wi' a' your days, the men you ha'e kept company wi', the men you ha'e . . .

She breaks down.

Oh, Wull, what made you dae it? We were happy. Ower happy. And noo we . . .

He comforts her.

Wull   We can be happy yet, Jenny. Let us gang awa' tigither. Awa' frae here. Here.

He hands **Jenny** *a ticket.*

Jenny   What is this?

Wull   I bought another ticket tae Canada. Come wae me. I cannae stay here any mair, they'll no' have me in the village. Let's both go tae Canada where nobody kens me, where we'll get peace.

Jenny   I never asked ye' tae dae that.

Wull   I ken ye' want tae go wi' me, Jenny.

Jenny   Ay, I want to go, I would love to see Canada, but I canna leave my family like this.

Wull   Forget your family. You've been dominated all your life. Jenny, break away from it. Defy them. You once told me ye' felt caged in Carhill, but it isn't the village that's caged you, it's your own folk in your own home.

Background, left to right: Hannah Donaldson, Tom McGovern, Anita Vettesse.
Foreground: Owen Whitelaw

Jenny   Dae ye' really think I am able to slip off wi' ye' after all that's happened?

Wull   I'm vexed for everything that's happened. It was for your sake I blacklegged. I wanted to get as much as take us awa' frae here.

Jenny   It's ower late, Wull. I canna forgi'e ye.

Wull   You're gey hard, Jenny.

Jenny   No, Wull, I'm no' hard, you played a gey hard game wi' *me*. Every dream and every hope shattered into a thousand bits.

Wull   It was the strike to blame, Jenny.

Jenny   Ay, the strike. The strike, has shattered oor hopes and broken oor he'rts.

Wull   We can be happy yet, Jenny.

Jenny   It's ower late, Wull.

Wull   The strike'll soon be forgotten.

Jenny   Ay, but you failed me. Failed us a'. *That* can never be forgotten.

Wull   I saw this in the pawn again.

He shows her the fiddle.

I wanted ye tae have it.

Jenny   Just because ye' want something doesn't mean ye always get it.

Wull   If I was to send for you after a while, Jenny . . .

Jenny   It's ower late, Wull. Guid-bye!

Wull   Think it ower for a while?

Jenny   Guid-bye!

Jock *and* **Jean** *enter and watch* **Wull** *leave.*

Jenny   Is the strike finished, Faither?

Jock   Finished, darlin', and we ha'e got knocked oot again. They have us working longer hours for nearly half the wage.

The company forms a chorus.

> I am the Common Man,
> I am the brute, and the slave,
> I am the fool, the despised,
> From the cradle to the grave.
>
> I am the hewer of coal;
> I am the tiller of soil;
> I am the serf of the seas,
> Born to bear and to toil.

I am the builder of halls;
I am the dweller of slums;
I am the filth and the scourge
When winter's depression comes.

I am the fighter of wars;
I am the killer of men;
Not for a day, or an age,
But again, and again, and again.

I am the Common Man;
But master of mine take heed,
For you have put into my head,
Oh! many a wicked deed.

Jean   Ay, but we're no' gaun to lose he'rt, Jock; we'll live to fight anither day; there's life in the auld dog yet. That's the spirit, my he'rties! Sing! Sing! Tho' they ha'e ye chained to the wheels and the darkness. Sing! Tho' they ha'e ye crushed in the mire. Keep up your he'rts, my laddies, you'll win through yet, for there's nae power on earth can crush the men that can sing on a day like this.

SONG 8: THE RED FLAG

The people's flag is deepest red,
It shrouded oft our martyred dead,
And ere their limbs grew stiff and cold,
Their hearts' blood dyed its ev'ry fold.

Then raise the scarlet standard high.
Within its shade we'll live and die,
Though cowards flinch and traitors sneer,
We'll keep the red flag flying here.

It well recalls the triumphs past,
It gives the hope of peace at last;
The banner bright, the symbol plain,
Of human right and human gain.

With heads uncovered swear we all
To bear it onward till we fall;
Come dungeons dark or gallows grim,
This song shall be our parting hymn.

*During 'The Red Flag' they dance. The men get faster and more
exhausted, they start to stumble, they continue until we are left with
exhausted workers staring at us.*

Left to right: Graham McLaren, Seth Hardwick.

Lightning Source UK Ltd.
Milton Keynes UK
UKOW05f0811021014

239472UK00011B/353/P